How to Win at Shopping

※[297]※

INSIDER SECRETS

FOR GETTING THE STYLE YOU WANT

AT THE PRICE YOU WANT TO PAY

DAVID ZYLA & EILA MELL

WORKMAN PUBLISHING • NEW YORK

This book is dedicated to those who love
and loathe shopping and to those who
create the wonderful world of retail!

. . . .

Copyright © 2015 by David Zyla and Eila Mell

All rights reserved. No portion of this book may be
reproduced—mechanically, electronically, or by any other
means, including photocopying—without written permission
of the publisher. Published simultaneously in Canada by
Thomas Allen & Son Limited.

Library of Congress Cataloging-in-Publication Data is
available.

ISBN 978-0-7611-8382-2

Design by Janet Vicario
Opener illustrations by Akane Nakamura
Spot illustrations by Lucia Bernard

Workman books are available at special discounts when
purchased in bulk for premiums and sales promotions as
well as for fund-raising or educational use. Special editions or
book excerpts can also be created to specification. For details,
contact the Special Sales Director at the address below or send
an email to specialmarkets@workman.com.

Workman Publishing Company, Inc.
225 Varick Street
New York, NY 10014-4381
workman.com

WORKMAN is a registered trademark of Workman Publishing
Co., Inc.

Printed in China
First printing January 2015

10 9 8 7 6 5 4 3 2 1

CONTENTS

INTRODUCTION

Have you ever gone into a swanky boutique and felt like Julia Roberts in *Pretty Woman*? Relax, you're not alone! Most of us have had these feelings of insecurity. The idea of shopping seems to divide people into two camps: those who love it and those who really don't. This book of shopping secrets is for both groups. For those of you who feel uncertain when stepping into a store, this is your game plan. We're confident it will quickly change your mind about the experience. And for all you fashionistas, you will love our insider tips. They'll prove to be indispensable additions to your current shopping skills.

No one is born knowing how to shop. It is an art that needs to be developed. You know that feeling of confidence you have when you're wearing your best outfit? You really can have that every day. We have made shopping super easy by breaking the process down for you. You'll understand how stores work, and why they're designed the way they are. Do you know why there is carpeting in certain areas? You will! Are you unsure of how a certain item should fit? You won't be any longer! Do you have trouble deciding when to make a purchase? Not a problem anymore!

We all have to shop. We want to give you the confidence you need to conquer any store and come away happy and with a fantastic wardrobe.

Shop Talk: Terms to Know

Brick-and-mortar store: A store that has a physical presence; a traditional store.

Cyber Monday: The online counterpart to Black Friday. Cyber Monday happens the Monday after Thanksgiving, and is an extremely busy day for online shopping.

Final sale: A sale item that cannot be returned or exchanged.

Flash sale: A sale with a high discount for a very limited amount of time.

Layaway: A purchasing method in which the customer can put an item on hold and pay for it in installments over time.

Markdown: The amount of money reduced from the price of an item.

↪

Markup: The amount of money added to the price of an item that covers the retailer's overhead and profit.

Pop-up store: A store that opens and closes in a short amount of time, from a day to a few weeks or months.

Presale: A sale that occurs before items are available to the public.

Price adjustment: If an item is bought at full price and then goes on sale within a short period of time (typically one to two weeks), the retailer may give the customer a price adjustment, or refund the difference.

Private label: A product for sale under the name of a retailer.

Sample sale: A sale of a designer's samples that were previously used to show new collections to retail buyers and fashion editors.

Shopworn clothes: Items with wear and tear from being displayed or handled in a store.

SKU: Short for Stock Keeping Unit, the SKU is a store's product and service identification code. Each style of clothing at every company has its own SKU.

CHAPTER ONE

Establishing a

Game Plan

Everything you need to know (and do) before you get to the store.

.... ⟫[1]⟪ ....

Before a major shopping trip, always go through the items in your closet that you purchased last season and never wore. It happens to the best of us. That incredible item you had to have has just hung in your closet, unworn. Taking stock of this before a shopping trip will give you pause before making another similar mistake. Take out all of the still-tagged items in your closet and try each one on. Look at yourself in the mirror, and write down at least three reasons you have yet to wear each piece. This list should go with you on your trip and be referenced whenever you contemplate a purchase.

⋅⋅⋅⋅⋅⋅⋅⋅⋅⋅⋅⋅⋅⋅⋅⋅⋅⋅⋅⋅⋅⋅⋅⋅⋅⋅⋅⋅ ⋙[2]⋘ ⋅⋅⋅⋅⋅⋅⋅⋅⋅⋅⋅⋅⋅⋅⋅⋅⋅⋅⋅⋅⋅⋅⋅⋅⋅⋅

Prior to shopping, always assess what
you need and remind yourself of what you
already own. It can be very frustrating buying
something only to realize later that you have a
similar item in your closet. This happens more
often than one would think. Many of us tend to
buy the same types of garments over and over
again. But really, how many black sweaters can
(and should) one have?

⋅⋅⋅⋅⋅⋅⋅⋅⋅⋅⋅⋅⋅⋅⋅⋅⋅⋅⋅⋅⋅⋅⋅⋅⋅⋅⋅⋅ ⋙[3]⋘ ⋅⋅⋅⋅⋅⋅⋅⋅⋅⋅⋅⋅⋅⋅⋅⋅⋅⋅⋅⋅⋅⋅⋅⋅⋅⋅

Sometimes the best shopping plan can come
from your current closet. No matter what
you think of your present wardrobe, it holds
many of your past triumphs. These pieces
and outfits should be used as clues to find the
perfect items you should be shopping for, ones
that are completely authentic to you. Think
of your clothes like costumes in a film you are
starring in. Ask yourself what they say about
your "character," then make sure that all future
purchases connect with and illustrate that vision.

·············· ≫[4]≪ ··············

Always snap photos of yourself wearing favorite items in your closet to use as visual reference on your shopping trip. The photos will not only inspire and influence your purchases, but they'll also help discern things like length, proportion, and fullness. Why wonder how the length of a skirt compares to your favorite back home when you can just reference a photo on your phone? This also works when shopping for accessories. There is no reason to question whether an accessory will complement an outfit when you can easily bring along a picture.

·············· ≫[5]≪ ··············

Collecting pictures from magazines and blogs and compiling your own "style file" will *always* open you up to shopping a wider array of looks. Start a folder, either physical or digital, with styles you like on others that might also work on you. You will begin to see patterns and will be able to more easily identify similar items when shopping.

.... ⟫[6]⟪ ....

Do some research before any and all shopping trips, and you will **always** have better results. Researching can save you time, money, and possible frustration. Searching online, making a phone call, or just asking around will help you discern which outlets are worth a long drive, the range of price points at a nearby department store, the probability of designer labels at a new consignment shop, or the opening time of an online flash sale.

.... ⟫[7]⟪ ....

If you suspect that specific branded items may be available at an outlet, research the quality and price of the pieces prior to your shopping trip. This will **always** enable you to make a faster decision. Knowing the full price will be extremely helpful, so you can compare it to the outlet price. If you are in any way disappointed with the item you came for, skip buying it. Your trip will not have been wasted, and neither will your money.

······························ ❋[8]❋ ······························

𝒜lways bring a bottle of water if you plan to
shop for a while. Shopping can be a workout.
There's walking, carrying armfuls of clothing
or packages, and trying clothes on. Who
wants to be slowed down by needing to find
a drink? Bring your own bottle and you won't
be interrupted.

······························ ❋[9]❋ ······························

For each and every shopping trip, always
plan to arrive looking like the best version
of yourself. Part of shopping is trying things
on, so you are going to be looking at yourself
repeatedly in a mirror. The face smiling back
should be the one that reflects how you feel at
your most attractive. Therefore, style your hair
the way you like it most, put on your number
one lipstick, and dab on some of your favorite
fragrance. When you are looking and feeling
your absolute best, it is much clearer to see
which clothes and accessories
connect with and complement you,
and which ones do not.

·····················≫[10]≪·····················

Never wear jewelry for a day of shopping.
Jewelry can make an outfit go from average
to extraordinary, but it can also be distracting.
When you're in the dressing room, it's best
that you see how new potential clothes and
accessories look on their own, without the
possible clash or embellishment of a statement
necklace or earrings. Also, it is very easy to
lose something when you're taking clothes on
and off. Avoid disappointment by leaving your
jewelry at home.

·····················≫[11]≪·····················

If you're spending the day at an outlet, always
wear clothing you can get in and out of easily.
You will spend much of your time trying things
on. A blouse you have to button and unbutton
twenty times will get annoying fast. Your best
outfit is something that comes on and off
easily. If you think of shopping like a sport,
plan your uniform for the fitting room.

....................✻[12]✻....................

Always wear comfortable shoes when outlet shopping. There will be a lot of walking. Wearing uncomfortable shoes will slow you down and shorten your day.

....................✻[13]✻....................

Never shop without time to do it thoroughly. Squeezing a shopping excursion in during your lunch hour can lead to a lot of stress. Waiting for a dressing room or parking space can add unexpected time to a shopping trip. Online shopping can be impeded by misplacing a password or having to start the checkout process over due to an expired shopping cart. And so on. When rushed, we often make decisions that we regret later. So put aside more time for shopping than you think you'll need. The best rule is to decide how much time you think you need, then add 25 percent more!

⁊[14]⁊

$\mathcal{N}$ever put off shopping for a special occasion until the last minute. Start a full month in advance. Otherwise you can easily end up spending more money, or getting something you don't love.

⁊[15]⁊

Shopping trips can sometimes be affected by your bad mood. There is a fifty-fifty chance that a shopping trip will lift your spirits. Finding a great piece at a wonderful price can cause endorphins and dopamine to be released in the brain and make you feel absolutely fantastic. However, if your current state leads you to reject everything that crosses your path, you will never get to that point. It might be better to postpone your trip until you are in better spirits.

How to Shop for
a Special Occasion

"When dressing for any special event, dress for yourself first. If you feel beautiful, you will *be* beautiful!"
—SUSAN LUCCI, *Emmy Award–winning actress*

✻ Pay attention to the formality listed on the invitation. Black tie means a formal short or long dress. For men, it means a tuxedo.

✻ Black tie preferred or optional means a formal dress, cocktail dress, or dressy separates. For men, it means a tuxedo or a dark suit.

✻ Semiformal means a cocktail dress or dressy separates. For men, a dark suit is appropriate.

✻ Festive attire means a cocktail dress, dressy separates, or any LBD (little black dress). For men, a jacket and tie will do the trick.

✻ Business formal means a business suit or dress. For men, a suit is appropriate.

✻ Business casual can be interpreted broadly, but don't wear anything overtly sexy.

✻ Casual dress means wear something you wouldn't mind being photographed in.

✻ When shopping for a wedding, don't choose anything that will compete with the bride.

·····················※[16]※·····················

$\mathcal{N}$ever feel that you have failed if you have an unsuccessful shopping day. From not having your size available at an online flash sale to trying on something that you were convinced would suit you and discovering that it does not, your success rate will vary through no fault of your own. The positive thing to draw from this experience is that you did not end up with anything that is going to hang unworn in your closet. Also, there is power in knowing what does not work for you, since it saves time and effort the next time!

·····················※[17]※·····················

$\mathcal{S}$ometimes setting an item limit each season will help you make more focused shopping choices. Deciding beforehand that you will get x number of pieces a season will actually help you choose the best items for you. It will also prevent you from ending up with a lot of pieces that you won't wear because you don't have anything to coordinate them with.

When to Break the Rules

"People who follow all the rules and chase every trend tend to be forgotten—they look great, but they're not as memorable."
—**DITA VON TEESE**

*A*s with all rules, there is a time and place when breaking them is appropriate, and at times even encouraged!

✳ The customer is *not* always right. Opening yourself up to new possibilities can be a great thing. You may go into a store with a clear idea of what you are looking for in terms of color, style, and fabric. A sales associate listens closely as you explain ... but then shows you something that is completely off track! Before reacting to the fact that the item is not what you asked for, ask him why he chose it for you. You might get an authentically objective opinion and end up adding something fresh and exciting to your closet.

✳ A change in your body sometimes dictates a change in shopping strategy. Gaining and losing weight is a natural occurrence, but it may alter the shopping rules you have established for yourself. If you discover that some shapes and silhouettes in your closet are no longer working for your body, it is time to schedule a fashion reboot. Head to a department store with a wide variety of merchandise, and dive in with a fresh fashion perspective. Think of yourself as a nudist who is discovering clothes for the first time, and try on each and every type of cut, silhouette, and neckline with an objective eye. Most important, do not omit styles and fits that have not worked previously. You will emerge with a plan and wardrobe to showcase your new body at its best.

✳ Sometimes when you are truly smitten with an item, rule breaking may lead to a new discovery. It may even seem contradictory to items that you have purchased in the past, but you absolutely love it! And you've stretched your wardrobe potential by purchasing something that you never would have even considered trying on before. Thus, the new discovery: You have found yet another perfect silhouette, cut, fabric, color, print, or metal to add to your shopping repertoire!

Be adventurous in the fitting room and experiment with varying cuts and necklines.

································❋[18]❋·····························

*A*lways set a spending limit if money is a concern. (And let's face it: Money is a concern for most people.) Setting a budget before a shopping trip will make you perfectly aware of what you can afford to spend. Just be sure to stick to it.

································❋[19]❋·····························

*A*lways remember that not all shopping is created equal. There are times when we go to browse, and there are times when we go to buy. When you intend to make a purchase, your shopping should be strategic. You have a goal, and it is to find fabulous things that make you look and feel your very best. Therefore, you should always do it with your full attention: Instead of shopping with your extra-chatty friend, meet her for dinner after a solo day at the mall, and do your online purchasing during the quiet hours when your children are in school or you aren't distracted. The results will be drastically better, and it will all be accomplished in much less time.

CHAPTER TWO

Strategic

SHOPPING

Conquering the
department store,
owning the outlet,
and going home with
a wardrobe you love.

DEPARTMENT STORES

................................※[20]※................................

A department store can sometimes be
overwhelming. If you go in knowing which
department you want to shop in, you can
overcome this feeling. You will also get less
distracted by items you see along the way, and
have a more focused and successful experience.

................................※[21]※................................

If you're going to shop multiple departments,
always take a look at the directory. You ↝

want to spend your time shopping, not wandering. By taking a quick look at the directory, you will be able to plan which departments to shop, and in what order. You will be more productive and less tempted by impulse items.

·····························⟩[22]⟨·····························

Always make note of which entrance you came in. Department stores have multiple entrances and exits. After a long day of shopping, it's easy to forget where you came in. Pay attention to the name of the entrance, as well as what department you came in through, to avoid getting lost (and potentially distracted) on the way out.

·····························⟩[23]⟨·····························

Always head directly for the item you went into the store for. If you are shopping for something specific, make that your goal. This is the best way to avoid overspending or going home without what you came for.

························≫[24]≪························

Store designers always have a plan to keep
you in a department for as long as possible.
Retailers never ever want you to be able to
take a quick browse which could easily result
in you thinking, "There is nothing here for me."
Instead, the plan is for you to be completely
immersed in a retail mecca full of shopping
stimulation on every hanger and shelf. Their
thinking is, the longer you stay, the more likely
you are to buy your way to the exit.

························≫[25]≪························

Studies have shown that upon entering a
store, people tend to go to the right side first.
Many items are chosen for purchase early on,
when people are still excited to be in the store,
and not yet tired. Therefore, the newest (and
the most expensive) merchandise is almost
always placed in the right side of a store or
department entrance. Keep this in mind and
you will be a savvier shopper.

························ ⟩[26]⟨ ························

Stores will **sometimes** use a concept known as "anchoring." Anchoring is a practice in which two similar items with very different price tags are placed next to each other. The more expensive item is placed there to get you think the less expensive one is a great deal.

························ ⟩[27]⟨ ························

Sometimes the layout, lighting, or music in a department store will affect your shopping success. Just as each of us has a specific aesthetic in clothing, we also have it in environments. It is quite possible that even though a store's merchandise could be perfect for you, the physical store experience does not have the same appeal. Try to separate the two by concentrating only on your shopping goals. Otherwise, you might cut your trip short and potentially pass up the absolutely perfect piece.

························⊰[28]⊱························

Always be aware of prices in carpeted areas of a store. Stores use carpeting to slow you down in the sections where they want you to spend the most time (and money). This is especially dangerous for parents with strollers.

························⊰[29]⊱························

Retailers will **sometimes** intentionally have a messy display to make an item seem more desirable. A disorderly display at the front of the store looks like everyone who has passed by has reached for that item, giving the impression that it is a must-have. It's also true the other way around. Retailers will sometimes discourage shopping the clearance section by keeping it messy.

························⊰[30]⊱························

Sometimes stores will deliberately design confusing displays or signs, such as "select merchandise on sale," which require sales ⤳

assistance. Research has found that shoppers who get help from a salesperson are more likely to make a purchase. If you need help deciphering a sign, by all means ask a salesperson. Just realize that this does not in any way obligate you to buy something.

·····························※[31]«·····························

Always scan a department for color first, then go in for a closer look at style, size, fabric, and price point. It's easy to get overwhelmed when approaching racks and racks of clothing. Color is the easiest starting point.

·····························※[32]«·····························

A department store will **sometimes** carry items that a designer namesake boutique does not, and vice versa. Don't be fooled into skipping a particular section in a department store because you already shopped at that designer's store. There will be some of the same merchandise, but there might also be enough different items to make it worth your while.

···≫[33]≪···························

Never shop an outfit exactly as a celebrity wore it. Rather, take a cue from the cut or color, and create your own iconic style. It's great to be inspired by someone else's outfit, but copying it head to toe is not in your best interest. What looks great on someone else may not work the same on you, and vice versa. Identify what attracts you about the outfit, then take the inspiration and make it your own. You will look equally good!

···≫[34]≪···························

Never buy something because it is the "It" item of the season. Every season has that one piece that everyone seems to own, but you do not need this item unless you absolutely love it. Buying something because it is the piece of the moment has "fashion victim" written all over it.

···················· ⁂[35]⁂ ····················

Treat your in-store shopping trip like a business meeting. *Never* distract yourself in the middle of it by answering a call on your phone. We realize this is tough for many people, especially parents. But this is your time for yourself. Unless there is a potential emergency, let the call go, and you can check the message at your convenience.

···················· ⁂[36]⁂ ····················

Strategic shopping with limited time is *always* better done solo. Everybody loves shopping with a friend. However, if you have limited time, another person will only slow you down. She will almost always want to stop to look at something. In addition, having a friend along will undoubtedly mean conversation, which will also take time away from shopping.

·····················❦[37]❦·····························

When shopping with a friend, *always* choose one who balances your shopping personality. Do you like to spend time going through every item on a rack, or do you quickly browse through? Make sure that your buddy has the same shopping personality as you, or one or both of you may get very frustrated during the excursion.

·····················❦[38]❦·····························

Never shop with a friend who tries to impose her own taste on you! We all have our own personal style. No one needs to shop with someone who doesn't recognize that, and who pressures you to get what she likes.

SALESPEOPLE

························※[39]※························

It's *sometimes* a smart move to politely decline when a salesperson asks to start a dressing room for you right away. Once you step into the fitting room, you are much more likely to make a purchase. Edit before you enter so that you only bring things into the fitting room that you are seriously considering buying.

························※[40]※························

Using a department store personal shopper is a free service that *never* has a minimum purchase requirement! Most department stores have personal shoppers who are available to navigate the store with you, free of charge. They know the merchandise and can easily guide you through the departments. Be sure to call in advance for an appointment.

·······················❧[41]❧·······················

Always create a nice relationship with an eager salesperson by replacing "I'm just browsing" with "I do not need help right now, but will find you when I do." This is a polite way to acknowledge a sales professional while making it clear that you would like to navigate the selling floor solo. Many sales associates are on commission or on a salary with incentives and rewards for reaching their sales goals. By responding in this manner, you are signaling that you understand this and will give them a sale, should there be one.

·······················❧[42]❧·······················

Other sizes may be as close as the stockroom, so *always* ask about the possibility! Don't walk away from a potentially perfect item because you do not see it in your size. The selling floor is typically only restocked before and after store hours, and size options can be severely depleted on busy days. If there is no one to ↝

ask about size availability in your immediate vicinity, take the garment in an incorrect size with you on your hunt for a sales associate. Once you find one, tell him your desired size and let him scan the item to see if it is in stock and which stockroom it may be located in.

························❧[43]❧························

Always expect a salesperson to check a nearby store if the requested full-priced item is not available at the current location in your size and color. Before asking for a stock check, determine your correct size by trying on a similar item, perhaps in another color. If the piece is available, you may have the option of requesting a store transfer or having your item held for pickup at the other location. If it is not, find out if the item may be available online.

·· ✻[44]✻ ··

Never expect a sales associate to special order or transfer a sale-priced item from another location. Fashion moves in one direction: forward. Once a season is done, there is a mad dash to get the leftovers out the door to make room for new merchandise. All concentration is on the current season. Stores make every effort to liquidate stock in each location rather than move things around from store to store.

·· ✻[45]✻ ··

Sometimes when a computerized stock system says an item is available in limited supply at another location, it is best to call to verify. Many of us champion shoppers will think nothing of traveling miles and miles for that must-have item the cashier said would be at another location. But the computerized stock system is not always up-to-date. So it ↬

can be extremely frustrating to arrive to find that the store is out of stock. You can avoid this situation by simply calling the store. If it does have your perfect item, let the store know you are on your way to buy it, and ask a salesperson to hold it for you until you arrive.

···※[46]※···

Always tell your salesperson if you're looking for a hard-to-find item. Some stores presell much of their inventory before it ever makes it to the selling floor. A salesperson will often know what is in the stockroom or about to hit the selling floor, so ask her for what you want. If the salesperson does not know, she can find out from the store buyer. A great salesperson will also know which other stores in the area might have the item, even if they're competitors.

·····················⊰[47]⊱·····················

Always ask for the business card of a sales associate you have enjoyed working with. Why start from scratch the next time you visit the store? Take the relationship a step further by sharing your information and ask for a call the next time items come in that he thinks you might like. Working with someone you know, and who knows your taste, can save you money. He will keep you updated on sales and promotions. You can also save time by calling ahead to let the sales associate know when you are coming in. He can preselect items and have them waiting for you in the dressing room.

·····················⊰[48]⊱·····················

Never be afraid to ask if an item will go on sale. Located in the stockroom or employee lounge of the store is a detailed calendar containing all of the upcoming promotions and sales. Ask your salesperson to take a peek at it. What can you lose?

∗[49]∗

Many sales professionals work on a commission basis, so *always* stay loyal to the ones you bond with! If you enter a store without spotting your prior salesperson and begin working with another one, you are unknowingly creating a potential conflict between associates. The person in front of you may not know that you have an established relationship with her colleague unless you tell her, so let the salesperson know up front. Continue with her only if the salesperson who has proved to be so helpful in the past is not in. When you're done shopping, make sure to ask the associate to send the absentee your best wishes. This makes it clear that you will stay loyal to your original salesperson and work with him the next time you are in.

·····················❧[50]❧·····················

$\mathcal{N}$ever feel pressured to buy just because the salesperson has spent a lot of time with you. Of course you may feel bad that he is not compensated with a big sale and commission for his time, but working in sales is a lot like prospecting. There are numerous factors that lead to a sale. Every seasoned salesperson knows that for the sake of repeat business, it is best to have you leave the store with only the items that you are absolutely sure about. Your primary shopping goal is to assemble a wardrobe of fantastic clothes and accessories that flatter you. It is not, however cold as it may sound, to personally support your salesperson. Think of shopping in black-and-white terms: Items either work in cut, color, fabric, size, and shape, or they do not, no matter who may be assisting you.

·····················※[51]※·····················

$\mathcal{N}$ever feel intimidated by a salesperson who is impeccably dressed. Instead, engage her. She may be able to turn her expert eye upon you and be extremely helpful. Many professional salespeople have gotten into the field because of their love of fashion and natural ability to put things together in interesting and innovative ways. If they can put themselves together brilliantly, might they be able to do the same for you? Find out by approaching the associate with a style compliment. Then share a little about your style and shopping goals, and see what happens.

·····················≫[52]≪·····················

Keep in mind that you **always** have the power
to purchase or pass. A salesperson is an expert
who is there to help you, but you should never
feel pressure from him to buy. If you find
his personality a bit overbearing or his style
advice contradictory to what feels right, do
not feel badly about politely excusing yourself.
Sales professionals, like all people, come in a
plethora of personalities, so find and work with
ones who mesh well with yours.

·····················≫[53]≪·····················

If you shop often and absolutely love the
merchandise at a local boutique, **always** ask
if you can meet and compliment the buyer.
It is always a good idea to let someone know
you appreciate her work. This may even
encourage her to think of you when ordering
for next season.

OUTLETS

························※[54]※························

Always get to outlet stores early. This is especially true during a sale. The earlier you arrive, the better chance you'll have of finding that great deal. You can also usually get a great parking spot!

························※[55]※························

Always park near the food court. This way, when you take a lunch break, you can put the morning's purchases in the trunk and start fresh for the afternoon. You will be relieved to not have to schlep your bags anymore, which can give you a boost of energy for the rest of the day. You can also easily pick up a snack or a drink for the ride home.

.... ⋇[56]⋇ ....

Always go to the most popular stores first. By noon they will be very crowded, and you may even have to wait on line to get in. These may be the stores you were most looking forward to. Why ruin the experience by having to squeeze through a crowd, wait on line for a fitting room (after waiting on line to enter the store in the first place), and deal with messy racks and shelves? Hit these stores when they first open, so you can breeze in and shop in peace.

.... ⋇[57]⋇ ....

Sometimes there is quite a bit of travel time required to get to an outlet. Never feel that you need to justify the drive by returning with bags full of things that aren't absolutely perfect for you. One great find is well worth the trip. Always remember to only buy something you absolutely *have* to have.

⋅⋅⋅⋅⋅⋅⋅⋅⋅⋅⋅⋅⋅⋅⋅⋅⋅⋅⋅⋅⋅⋅⋅⋅⋅⋅⋅⋅⋅⋅⋅≫[58]≪⋅⋅⋅⋅⋅⋅⋅⋅⋅⋅⋅⋅⋅⋅⋅⋅⋅⋅⋅⋅⋅⋅⋅⋅⋅⋅⋅⋅⋅⋅⋅

Outlet stores sometimes have merchandise specifically made for them. This does not mean that the item isn't good quality. It just means that it was never part of the line that went to the retail stores. Keep in mind that these items might not be returnable at the brand's non-outlet store.

⋅⋅⋅⋅⋅⋅⋅⋅⋅⋅⋅⋅⋅⋅⋅⋅⋅⋅⋅⋅⋅⋅⋅⋅⋅⋅⋅⋅⋅⋅⋅≫[59]≪⋅⋅⋅⋅⋅⋅⋅⋅⋅⋅⋅⋅⋅⋅⋅⋅⋅⋅⋅⋅⋅⋅⋅⋅⋅⋅⋅⋅⋅⋅⋅

Never let the "full price" number on an outlet price tag influence a purchasing decision. We all love getting a great deal, but there are other factors when deciding to make a purchase. Always concentrate on whether the current price is in line with how great the item looks on you. Keep in mind that even if something is deeply discounted, it still may be too expensive at that particular time. If you feel stressed about the price, don't buy it.

·····················❦[60]❦·····················

Price tags are **sometimes** misleading. Unless clearly marked "original price," items at a discount store may not ever have been offered at the amount listed. Sometimes retailers will claim that a particular price is the "discount" price when it's really just the regular price of the item. It is also possible that the items were manufactured for the discount store. The tags could also say something vague like "offered elsewhere at . . ." However, none of these reasons should interfere with your decision making. It is best to remember that if the item suits you perfectly and the price is what you want to pay for it, then make it yours.

·····················❦[61]❦·····················

Never pass by a rack of "factory seconds" without a quick glance. These are items that did not pass inspection, but their defects could be as minor as a slight snag hidden by a belt. It may be worth your while since the discounts are always deep.

TOP TEN
Wardrobe Staples

"Staples have a strange way of staying intact on the shelf—like a large box of cereal. I'm a believer in buying less and coordinating your clothes to mix and match!"
—**BETTY HALBREICH,** *Solutions by Betty Halbreich, Bergdorf Goodman*

✷ It is always a good idea to have a well-fitting pair of trousers. They work for so many occasions.

✷ A great pair of jeans can act as a neutral to many other things in your closet.

✷ An A-line skirt will always flatter.

✷ A pencil skirt can make the most basic blouse super sexy.

✷ You can never go wrong with a dress in your best, darkest neutral—your personal LBD.

✷ A crisp shirt in your version of white will never be a waste of money.

✷ A blazer in a neutral color will complement many outfits.

✷ A stylish pair of flats can be your feet's best friend.

✷ A pair of classic pumps will work with almost anything.

✷ A piece of statement jewelry will always liven up a simple outfit.

............................⁂[62]⁜............................

Consider outlet shopping during off-peak hours. It is easier to navigate an outlet when it is not crowded, you will always be able to cover more ground in less time, and you may also have the advantage of shopping freshly arrived merchandise. There will also be shorter lines, which can really speed you up. And there is no greater motivation than the idea of getting something as it hits the rack.

AT THE REGISTER

............................⁂[63]⁜............................

Items displayed at the register are always placed there to tempt you. These small, mostly inexpensive items are there so that you will throw them in with the rest of your haul at the last minute, without having time to properly think the purchase through.

·······························※[64]※·······························

Sometimes it's worth waiting before you buy. If you have the time and patience to wait, your items may get marked down or go on sale.

·······························※[65]※·······························

Never buy an item you don't love. Your money and closet space are not worth sacrificing for anything you don't love. A wardrobe of only items you love will guarantee you a great outfit every day.

·······························※[66]※·······························

Sometimes the best way to avoid owning an impulse purchase is to simply pause before you purchase it. Give yourself a twenty-four-hour period to see if you remember it enough to go back for it. If you're unsure, walk away. If you can't stop thinking about it, go back to the store. Otherwise, you're probably better off without it. You can also ask the store to put the item on hold for twenty-four hours.

··≫[67]≪·····························

As a budgeting monitor, **always** pay with cash when shopping in a brick-and-mortar store. It's so easy to whip out your credit card and worry about paying later. However, if you pay with cash, you will most likely spend 20 to 50 percent less than when shopping with a credit card.

··≫[68]≪·····························

𝒩ever spend more than you can afford. It's easy to get seduced by fabulous merchandise, but never, ever buy something you can't afford. No item is worth getting in financial trouble for. If you feel you must have the piece, then save up for it and buy it when you can swing it.

··≫[69]≪·····························

𝒩ever open a store credit card. Opening a credit card should be your idea, and not something you decide on the spot because a cashier says you can save 10 percent on ↪

your purchase. The interest rates on these cards are typically through the roof and not worth it. Stick to your own card, especially one where you earn points or get cash back.

·····························❊[70]❊·····························

Always check the return policy, whether online or in-store. Just because the standard return period is thirty days doesn't mean that is always the case. You may find that you only have twenty-one or seven days. Then there's the dreaded "exchange only" policy. Simply ask what the return policy is at checkout, and you won't be surprised later.

·····························❊[71]❊·····························

When offered a garment bag and hanger, *always* accept. A garment bag will always come in handy, so why turn it down? It's such a great way to store items you wear seasonally or just on special occasions. You can tape a picture of the item on the garment bag so you know what's inside without unzipping.

How to Shed Ten Pounds

JUST BY GETTING DRESSED

"To achieve a long and lean proportion, above all, don't cut yourself in half!"

—**PATRICIA FIELD**, *stylist/fashion designer*

＊ While a straight skirt can be slimming, the effect can go awry if the bottom hem abruptly stops without tapering back to the leg, creating an unflattering horizontal line. If a straight skirt or dress hangs like a lampshade, consider a trip to the tailor.

＊ When fitting a jacket, consider narrowing the sleeves to separate the arms from the torso. This will create a more streamlined silhouette.

＊ When shopping for a jacket, make sure that the waist is defined.

＊ When shopping for pants, reach for ones with a Hollywood-style waist with a side or back zipper, and not ones that are pleated or full in the leg.

＊ When shopping for separates, avoid high-contrast tops and bottoms that chop the body up. Instead, look for low-contrast or monochromatic combinations.

＊ Extra fabric often adds visual bulk. Think fitted when shopping and pass on the bell sleeves, softly draped dresses, and full pleated skirts.

* Showing a bit more skin can be a great idea. When it comes to fabric on the body, less fabric is more slimming.

* Avoid wearing fabrics with sheen on the parts of the body you would like to de-emphasize. Sheen will make those areas appear larger. Instead, think of such fabrics as a fantastic way to illuminate the smaller parts of your body and balance the head-to-toe look.

* Shadow the waist by buying a skinny belt in a darker version of the color of your outfit, or in a contrasting dark neutral.

* Shop wider, vertical stripes, which will elongate the body, rather than horizontal ones, which will broaden it.

* With shoes, a low vamp will start the leg line at a lower point, thus creating a longer, leaner look.

* Buy a long cardigan, necklace, or scarf to add a strong vertical quality to every outfit—the effect will elongate the body.

* The higher the heel, the leaner the look, so consider shopping shoes two-and-a-half inches or higher. Also consider the fact that a skinny spike won't balance the proportion of a fuller calf or ankle, so reach for a thicker, shapelier heel instead.

* The best go-to slimming piece is a figure-flattering dress in a dark neutral. If you find one in the perfect style, color, and fabric, don't hesitate to spend a bit more on it. You will feel so good in it that the amount of use will justify the purchase.

* The right shapewear can make you appear slimmer because it actually *does* work.

·······························≫[72]≪·····························

If you're hesitant about a purchase, always hold on to the receipt. Set and name an alarm on your phone for one day prior to the last return date. It's so easy to forget to get back to the store for a return. However, if you don't, you will have a reminder of your bad decision staring you in the face every time you open your closet. Closet space is precious. Don't fill it up with clothes you'll never wear. Setting an alarm is the best way to ensure that you return your item and get your money back.

·······························≫[73]≪·····························

If you find yourself always returning things, perhaps consider the root causes. Are they practical or psychological? Returns are perfectly common. But if you are returning items on a regular basis, you are not making the best choices while shopping. Think back and make a list of the reasons for your returns. You will most likely see a pattern, and can address it on future shopping outings.

···················· ⁂[74]⁂ ····················

A smart purchase is **always** something you can wear in multiple ways and with many different items in your closet. You will end up needing less clothing if you buy items that follow this rule. Remember, you don't need a closet jam-packed with clothes. You need a closet full of clothes you wear.

···················· ⁂[75]⁂ ····················

Never feel guilty about coming up empty-handed from a shopping trip. It can be frustrating to spend a day shopping with nothing tangible to show for it. However, you have actually been very smart. It's always better to wait for something that you're in love with and makes you shine rather than settling for something that is just okay.

·····························❋[76]❋·····························

There is a limited amount of space in even the
largest closets. If you return from a successful
shopping trip and don't have room to fit your
purchases, *always* swap out one item that you
have not worn in a year or more for each of
your new ones. It is not a good idea to overstuff
a closet. You won't be able to see what you
have, and your clothing will get wrinkled just
by hanging there. If you don't have room to
move the hangers, your closet is too full.

CHAPTER THREE

FINDING YOUR PERFECT MATCH

in the

Fitting Room

**Deciding which fit,
style, and color you want
to go home with.**

................................⟫[77]⟪................................

Never buy anything in a brick-and-mortar
store without trying it on first. Even a duplicate
of something you currently own could be
mismarked. To avoid possible returns, take an
extra couple of minutes and try everything on.

................................⟫[78]⟪................................

Always use a three-way mirror if one is
available. Not everyone likes to leave the
privacy of their dressing room and make their
way to the communal three-way mirror at the
end of the hall. It is well worth it, however,
since there is no better way to get a look
at yourself from every angle. You are doing
yourself a disservice by not making use of this
if it is available to you.

.... ❧[79]❧ ....

Always sit down in clothes you're trying on. An item may look great when you're standing up straight, but it is also worth seeing how it looks and feels when you're seated. After all, you'll be spending time sitting down in everything you buy. Most fitting rooms have seating, so this is easy to do.

.... ❧[80]❧ ....

Never dismiss something you love because the designer's sizing requires you to go up one size! We can't stress enough that there are no standard sizes. One designer's 4 can be another designer's 6. Do not feel bad if you have to go up a size for a particular garment. As long as the clothing you currently own still fits, you are the same size as always.

························≫[81]≪························

Stitching that bunches up or puckers is always a sign of poor quality, and is not worth your money. It only takes a few seconds to check the stitching on a garment. No matter how cute something is, if the stitching is problematic or suspicious, you can be assured the item won't last very long.

························≫[82]≪························

Lining can sometimes hide the quality of a garment. We've all been conditioned to think a lined garment is a quality garment. However, sometimes a lining can mask imperfections. Do not assume an item is worth your money merely because it is lined, especially if the lining is puckered or bunched.

························≫[83]≪························

Sometimes a store's private label will rival the quality of the designer label. Oftentimes, the reasonably priced private-label piece is made in the same factory as the one with the hefty ↝

designer price tag. Consider the private label for your basic items. You will get the same quality and avoid paying more for the status of the designer label.

················· ※[84]※ ·················

Never pass on a piece because you have not heard of the brand. There are an incredible number of fantastic designers out there who are not household names. Be open to trying on things from new designers. If it works on you, it is the perfect brand!

················· ※[85]※ ·················

When shopping, you should *always* make a habit of comparing all potential new items with the most-complimented item in your closet. Take your cues from what you know works. Is it the neckline, cut, or color? Being aware of what you look great in—and why— will inform your future purchases and help you build a fabulous wardrobe.

························ ❈[86]❈ ························

Sometimes a second opinion from a fellow shopper or sales associate can make your decision to purchase clearer. While shopping alone, don't be shy about asking a stranger for a second opinion if you doubt an item. The advantage to consulting the salesperson is that she's seen many people try on the merchandise. She can easily tell if it's right on you. The downside is that she may be working on commission, and therefore motivated to make the sale. We love the idea of asking a fellow shopper. Just make sure to ask someone you consider well dressed.

························ ❈[87]❈ ························

Never disregard something because the fit isn't perfect. While it is extremely important that your clothing fits properly, keep in mind that simple things like hem and sleeve length can be fixed by a tailor. Just factor in the cost of alterations to the cost of the garment to decide if it is still worth the price.

·····························※[88]※·····························

Always ask if a store has free alterations. How often does something fit perfectly straight off the rack? Some department stores offer free alterations, so find out if yours does and take advantage of this fantastic service.

·····························※[89]※·····························

Familiarize yourself with the fees charged by outside tailors so that you can *always* compare them with fees charged by a department store or boutique. Alterations are important, but you don't want to overpay.

·····························※[90]※·····························

Always go up a size to appear slimmer. Many of us would like to be as small a size as possible. However, nothing will add pounds faster than clothes that are too tight. (This is how the dreaded muffin top happens.) When deciding between two sizes, go for the slightly larger one.

························*[91]*························

Never buy anything that will fit after you lose *x* amount of weight. It is fine to want to lose a few pounds. But if you are shopping, it's important to buy what fits you now. Buying something with the thought that it will inspire you to lose weight doesn't work and can be a waste of money.

························*[92]*························

Never buy an itchy sweater or any uncomfortable item. Certain pieces of clothing can be so tempting, making it all the more disappointing when you try them on and find that, while they look great, they don't *feel* especially good. Do not be lured into the purchase. No matter how great it looks, if it bothers you after wearing it for a few minutes, can you imagine wearing it for an entire day?

[93]

When trying on a button-down shirt, **always** stretch your arms back so that your chest sticks out. If the buttons gape, don't buy it, as you will almost certainly inadvertently flash your bra at some point.

[94]

Three-quarter sleeves are **always** flattering on *all* body types. They work on everyone because they hit at the narrow part of the arm—and they also draw attention to the slimmest part of the waist!

[95]

The texture of ribbed tops will **always** make you look bigger on top, which is good news for some and not others. Women with small busts can embrace them, while those with larger busts may want to pass.

WHAT A TAILOR
Can and Can't Do

> "It is only fitting that I rely on good tailors to help make my designs come to life on the stage."
> —**WILLIAM IVEY LONG,** *six-time Tony Award–winning costume designer*

CAN

✳ Add top stitching back to the hem of your jeans after shortening.

✳ Maximize the amount of length in a pair of pants by dropping the hem to the longest possible length and finishing the inside with hem tape.

✳ Stitch down and remove the front pockets of your pants to create a smoother, slimmer effect.

✳ Shorten straps so that a dress or top raises to fit through the torso and has properly placed bust darts and underarms.

✳ Shorten sleeves. If your coat sleeve is past the knuckle or your blazer sleeve is past the wrist, they can be adjusted.

✳ Line a sheer garment with your shade of nude (the color most complementary to your skin tone) to enable you to wear regular undergarments under it.

✳ Add a hook and eye or snap at the point where your button-front blouse gapes.

CAN'T

* Take more than two inches out of the back center seam of jeans or pants with back pockets. Otherwise, the pockets will be too close together.

* Let out the seams of a garment made of a fabric that will show stitch marks such as linen, cotton, or silk. The result would be holes in your clothes.

* Reduce something more than one size. The proportions and seams will not end up where they should be.

* Remove heavy shoulder pads from a jacket. The fabric will not drape or fit your shoulders correctly without them.

* Lengthen a jacket. Shortening may be possible, but there will not be enough seam allowance to lengthen.

* Repair a hole by stitching it closed. Avoid a lumpy outcome and ask for a recommendation for a reweaving service.

* Change the original design completely. Alterations are possible, but if transformation is desired, go for another garment or have something custom made.

··≥[96]≤··

*N*ever buy a jacket that doesn't fit in the shoulders. There are many things a tailor can take care of. The shoulders of a jacket should not be one of them. If the shoulder seam doesn't sit right at your shoulders, find another jacket.

··≥[97]≤··

*A*lways button all the buttons when trying on a blazer. Although you probably won't wear it this way, it's a good way to check out the fit. If the blazer pulls, it's too small. If it sags, it's too big.

··≥[98]≤··

You can **sometimes** spend less on items such as T-shirts, blazers, or knits by shopping in the boys' department. Yes, ladies, it is possible to score fantastic finds. Keep in mind, though, this is never going to be the case for pants. Shop the boys' department, but make sure you get the proper fit.

························ ⁂[99]⁂ ························

𝒜lways remember that suits, twinsets, or anything that comes with more than one piece can—and should—also be worn as separates. Suits and sets are great: You have a ready-made outfit. However, don't forget that these pieces are not glued together. Break them up and wear them all separately. Just be sure to wash the pieces together, otherwise the color may not stay the same.

························ ⁂[100]⁂ ························

𝒩ever rule out a jacket or top because it has shoulder pads. Shoulder pads can be great, but they are not for everyone. If you don't need the extra padding, have a tailor remove them. Just be aware that this won't work with bulky or heavy shoulder pads since removing them will result in loose, sagging shoulders that will alter the look considerably from the designer's intentions.

························ ❧[101]❧ ························

Sometimes a logo can overwhelm the wearer and enter the room before the person does. Your body is not a billboard. Be aware of the power of a logo, and unless a brand is paying you to endorse it, think twice before wearing it.

························ ❧[102]❧ ························

When debating purchasing an item, always go back to the question "How do *I* look in the garment?" You may love an item you saw on a red carpet or in a magazine, but unless you love it on you, there is no reason to buy. Chances are, if you're questioning it, it's for a reason.

························ ❧[103]❧ ························

Never be afraid to try something on. You see something avant-garde and intriguing in your size at a great price. Would you wear this? Could you wear this? Try it on! There is zero risk in taking something outside your comfort zone into the fitting room. If it looks silly, ↪

that's the end of it. However, you may discover that it suits you, and you'll have found a great treasure.

.... ❈[104]❈ ....

Sometimes thinking of which character in a movie might wear a certain garment may help you make the final decision. It can be helpful to think like a costume designer if you're unsure. Decide what fictional character a garment would work on, and then you can decide if it feels like you. If it reflects you, make the purchase. If not, pass.

.... ❈[105]❈ ....

Never blame your body if a garment doesn't fit. We know how it feels to spend a day trying things on with nothing fitting right. It can seem like your body is the problem. This is never the case. It only means that the models used for the lines you have been trying on are a different body type than you. Not better—different.

······················· ☀[106]☀ ·······················

Always remember that your clothing should be used to showcase you, so let go of all size and label tags. No one is checking the labels in your clothing when you're not looking. Don't worry about what size a garment is, or who the designer is. The important things are: Does it flatter you? And is it good quality?

······················· ☀[107]☀ ·······················

When trying things on, you should easily be able to discern the "yes" from the "no" items. If you come across one that stumps you, **never** waste time staring at it. Take it off and place it in a "maybe" pile. Continue your try-ons, and return to the "maybe" again after putting on your favorite "yes" of the day. See if it belongs in the same category!

HOW TO SHOP FOR
a Job Interview

"To make a good first impression, choose clothes that allow you to come across as the very best, most authentic version of yourself."
—**CAROL SAWDYE**, *Vice Chairman and Chief Financial Officer, PwC*

✳ Shop for two items in your best color: one for the initial interview and one for the second. Repeating the color the second time will remind them of why they liked you the first time.

✳ Go for a classic item, such as a pencil skirt, a shift dress, or a great pair of trousers.

✳ Make sure your outfit is tailored to telegraph your level of polish and expertise.

✳ Don't necessarily listen to a friend's advice for an interview outfit if she doesn't work in the field. Her frame of reference may be limited to how she has seen your profession portrayed on television.

✳ Get a nice bag. You don't have to break the bank; just make sure it looks professional. And keep it neat so you're never digging through your bag to find something.

✳ You cannot go wrong with a medium heel.

JEANS

·························· ❧[108]❧ ··························

It is **sometimes** necessary to try on a stack of jeans in order to find the perfect pair. We understand that buying jeans can be tough. It's seldom that someone finds denim perfection right away. It's common to try on twenty-plus pairs until you find the right one for you. Don't be discouraged. You will find them, and be very happy when you do. After you determine which jeans fit you best, you can always go back to that brand or style when you need a new pair.

·························· ❧[109]❧ ··························

Always bend down when trying on jeans. Try bending at the knees and at the waist. If you can't do this comfortably, you're in the wrong pair.

···················· ❧[110]❧ ····················

Always sit or squat in jeans to see how well they fit. Even if you are a plumber, if your tush is peeking through, go for a different pair.

···················· ❧[111]❧ ····················

Never buy jeans that are loose in the crotch. A baggy crotch is not a good look on anyone. Always make sure your jeans fit properly without being too tight, either.

···················· ❧[112]❧ ····················

Always pay attention to the waistband when shopping for jeans. Slide two fingers into the waistband. If it is hard to do, the jeans are too tight. If it's too easy, they're too loose.

···················· ❧[113]❧ ····················

A darker wash jean will *always* be more slimming. Just like a well-fitting LBD, a dark jean in a classic cut is infinitely flattering.

·························· ⊰[114]⊱ ··························

Trouser jeans will always work on all body types. They will fit you like a great pair of pants. Buy them in a dark wash, and you can wear them at most occasions to which you would wear nice trousers.

·························· ⊰[115]⊱ ··························

Whiskering in denim will always draw attention to the part of the body it's on. You know those white lines going across your jeans horizontally? Those are whiskers. They will draw the eye, so take note of where they're placed. They are also horizontal stripes, which can widen you.

·························· ⊰[116]⊱ ··························

Never buy a pair of jeans because they are the brand of the moment. There is no reason to be a slave to trends. The most stylish women take into account what's happening at the moment, but will only wear what's right on them. If there's an "It" item that doesn't suit, ↪

they will skip it. It is much smarter to buy a pair of jeans that works for your body, rather than getting the hot new pair.

·················· ⁅ 117 ⁆ ··················

$\mathcal{N}$ever buy a pair of jeans if the zipper is pulling. If the zipper looks like it may open at any moment, that is a clear sign you need to go up a size.

·················· ⁅ 118 ⁆ ··················

$\mathcal{A}$lways beware of jeans with too much stretch. A little stretch is a great thing. However, if your jeans have too much, they may lose their shape after a few washings.

·················· ⁅ 119 ⁆ ··················

If there is a gap between your body and the jeans' waistband, they will **never** fit well. You can try going down a size, but you may just need a different brand. If you find this to be a problem with multiple brands, then try a different style.

UNDERGARMENTS

.... ❊[120]❊ ....

A bra that fits properly will **never** be uncomfortable. No matter how beautiful a bra is, what good is it if it doesn't fit? A bra should be an item of clothing you put on and forget you're wearing. You should not have to tug at or adjust it during wear.

.... ❊[121]❊ ....

Never buy a bra that is too small, or you'll look like you have four boobs. We cannot stress enough how unflattering this can be. It sets a poor foundation for any garment you layer over it, and just makes it apparent to anyone who sees you that your bra is too tight.

⋇[122]⋇

Never buy a bra without trying it on, even if you have other bras from the same company. It would stand to reason that if one bra from a company fits, then the same size from the same company would fit as well. That is not the case! There are so many different styles of bras; a full coverage bra may work for you, but one with a front closure may not. Try them all on to ensure the right fit.

⋇[123]⋇

Always get a professional bra fitting every two years, or any time your weight changes significantly. This is the number one rule of bras! Although we have all seen countless charts educating us on how to determine our bra size, it's worth going to a professional. Those charts can be confusing, and you do not want to get this wrong. Go to the lingerie section of any department store, or go to a lingerie shop and tell them you'd like a fitting. It is always free, so there is no reason not to.

········· ≫[124]≪ ·········

If a cup puckers, your bra is too big. You should **always** fill out your cup, without spilling over. If there is puckering, it simply means there is too much fabric. Go down a cup size!

········· ≫[125]≪ ·········

Never rely on a bra's shoulder straps as the main source of support. That is the job of the band. Your shoulder straps should only *help* support you. Try slipping off the shoulder straps when trying on a bra. If there is a noticeable lack of support, the bra does not fit.

········· ≫[126]≪ ·········

Always go up a band size if the shoulder straps are too tight. You should never have welts on your shoulder after a day in your bra. To avoid deep indentations in your skin, and the pain that goes with them, pay close attention to this detail while you're trying on bras. If there is any discomfort at all, you need a larger band size.

·························· ∦[127]∦ ··························

Always go down a band size if your bra straps fall off your shoulders at the tightest setting. For example, if you're in a 36, try a 34. You can keep the same cup size, however.

·························· ∦[128]∦ ··························

Always try on bras using the loosest hook. We've heard it a hundred times: Try your bra on using the middle hook. Who decided this? Bras stretch out over time. If your bra fits at the loosest setting, you can tighten it over time to maintain the right fit and extend the life of your bra.

·························· ∦[129]∦ ··························

A bra is *always* too big if it feels like your bust may bust out the bottom. There is never a circumstance where this is okay. Not only is it extremely uncomfortable, it also means your bra is not doing its basic job of supporting you. Try on a smaller one!

························· ❧[130]❧ ·························

You may **sometimes** need a different size in a
strapless bra. Strapless bras can be tricky. Even
if your regular bra is from the same company as
your strapless, it may still fit slightly differently.
It's always worth the extra few minutes to try
on the strapless in a range of sizes.

························· ❧[131]❧ ·························

Never rule out a backless dress just because
you need the support of a bra. A backless dress
can be forbidden fruit for women with large
busts who need support. However, there is
no need to despair. There are many options
available, including low-back longline bras and
adhesive bras.

························· ❧[132]❧ ·························

A nude bra is **always** a good idea because it
works under almost everything—even a white
top. A bra in a color closest to your skin tone
should be your default.

························ ❋[133]❋ ························

$\mathcal{N}$ever wear a white bra under a black top. In bright light, your white bra will be visible underneath dark colors—not a good look, and people will definitely notice.

························ ❋[134]❋ ························

A black bra is always best under a black top. It makes perfect sense: A black bra will always disappear under a black top (or dress). Keep in mind, though, that this is not the case for other color combinations!

························ ❋[135]❋ ························

A strapless bra without an underwire will sometimes give you a uniboob. In most cases, it's a good idea to stick with strapless bras with underwires. A bandeau may be super comfy, but nobody wants to look like they have one big pillow strapped across their chest. If you are larger than an A cup, it may also not give you enough support.

·············· ⁂[136]⁂ ··············

*A*lways remember that celebrities on the red carpet are wearing shapewear, and you can, too. Some celebs will even double up on it for an extra-slim appearance. We do not recommend this. One is fine! Besides offering a sleek appearance, it will also rid you of any potential panty lines.

·············· ⁂[137]⁂ ··············

*N*ever buy underwear that is too small. Too-tight panties will be uncomfortable, distracting (we are all too busy to have to adjust our underwear throughout the day), and it creates bulges beneath your clothing.

·············· ⁂[138]⁂ ··············

Shapewear panties can **sometimes** make you look bigger. Here's the deal: Shapewear panties will push everything up, which may create a roll over the top of your waistband that will be visible from under your clothes. Instead, ↪

invest in a shapewear bodysuit, even if you only need the help on the bottom.

·························· ❧[139]❧ ··························

Shapewear can **sometimes** be hazardous to your health! Never buy shapewear that is too small in the hope it will make you look smaller. It is dangerous to spend a long time in something that is too tight. You also do not want to wear shapewear on a very hot day. It is typically not made of breathable fabrics and can hold in more heat. To avoid your day or evening being interrupted by EMTs, forgo shapewear when the temperature rises.

·························· ❧[140]❧ ··························

Sometimes thongs are not the choice for everyone. There are definitely two kinds of women: those who love thongs, and those who hate them. If you hate them, don't wear them. It is not worth it to be uncomfortable, and there are plenty of other choices out there.

································ ❧[141]❧ ································

VPLs are **never** cute. Your best bet to avoid visible panty lines is to wear seamless underwear or a thong, or smooth them out with shapewear.

Shoes

································ ❧[142]❧ ································

Always bring shoes into the fitting room. Shoes can make an outfit. Why imagine how you would look with the right shoes when the store will most likely have a similar pair you can throw on? It's a common practice for stores to have them on hand, and the salesperson can easily accommodate you.

································ ❧[143]❧ ································

Always shop for shoes in the afternoon. Have you ever noticed that your shoes fit better sometimes? Weather can be a factor, as well ↪

as the time of day. Your feet swell during the day, so buying shoes in the afternoon, when your feet are at their largest, will make you less likely to wind up with shoes that don't fit properly.

.... ⁂[144]⁂ ....

Never buy shoes that don't fit. We can't stress this enough. No matter how great a shoe looks or how fantastic a sale is, you should absolutely never buy a pair of shoes that doesn't fit. If your foot slides around when you walk, the shoe is too loose. If you can't move your toes at all, your shoes are too tight and can be damaging to your feet. After all, if you have foot problems, you won't be able to wear certain types of shoes at all, including most heels.

.... ⁂[145]⁂ ....

Always peel and stick padded inserts into your completely flat shoes to ensure day-long comfort if you need extra arch support. They are wonderful and can make it possible to spend extra comfortable hours in your shoes.

[146]

Shoes that are a half-size too big can **sometimes** be made to fit with a pad or an insole. You never want to wear shoes that are the wrong size. However, if they are just slightly too big, a pad at the back of the ankle can help them to fit perfectly. An added bonus is that the pad will bring you comfort.

[147]

Shoes that are tight across the bridge can **always** be stretched if they're made of soft natural leather or fabric. When we say tight across the bridge, we mean a little bit tight. If you feel like one of Cinderella's stepsisters, then the shoe is too small. If it just about fits, though, you can stretch the soft leather or natural fabric for a great fit.

[148]

Shoes that hurt when you first try them on will **never** be transformed into comfortable ones, even with pads, stretching, insoles, etc. If a ↪

shoe gives you pain, it is never going to be a good shoe for you. You will also find that if your shoes hurt, you won't wear them anyway, no matter how gorgeous they are. This will be a waste of money, so move on to the next pair.

Shoes with soles that are sewn on, rather than glued on, are always better quality. Buy the best-quality shoes you can afford, since at their most basic level they are protective wear. Take a look at how the heel is attached for a big clue about the quality. No one wants to get caught mid-commute having to remove a shoe because the glue dried out and the heel cracked off. Bottom line: A stitched-on sole will always be the better buy.

·········· [150] ··········

Always feel inside a shoe with your hand to make sure it is smooth and comfortable. If there are any unexpected bumps, choose another pair. You can avoid so much discomfort this way.

·········· ❧[151]❧ ··········

A wider heel *always* means a more comfortable shoe. There is a reason there are no stiletto sneakers. A wide heel will help distribute weight more evenly. If you have a long day on your feet and need to wear heels, your best buy is a wide heel.

·········· ❧[152]❧ ··········

Always spend a few minutes walking around the store in shoes you're considering buying. Your shoes may slip on easily enough, but will you be comfortable walking around in them all day long? You're not going to know for sure until you do, but if you walk around the store in the shoes you're considering, you'll have a much better sense of how comfortable they will be.

·········· ❧[153]❧ ··········

When it comes to shoes, all is not *always* apparent in the store. After deciding the comfort level of your new heels in the ↪

store, try wearing them around the house before any extended period of time outside so you still have the option of returning them if necessary. Try wearing them for a few hours and try them on different floor surfaces to make sure you're happy with them.

·················· ⁕[154]⁕ ··················

Always look at shoes in a full-length mirror. Those little shoe mirrors will not give you the full picture. You already know how the shoe looks on your foot. What you want to see is what the shoe does for your entire body: how it looks with your clothes, as well as what it does for your posture.

·················· ⁕[155]⁕ ··················

The best toe shape will always match your best neckline. If a V-neck works for you, try a pointy-toed shoe. If you like a scoop neck, reach for a round-toe shoe. Try it out; you may love the results!

.... ❧[156]❧ ....

Always avoid ankle straps if your goal is to create a long, lean head-to-toe line. Ankle straps can be super cute. However, they will call attention to your ankles and break that line. Tall women can get away with this much more easily than petite women.

.... ❧[157]❧ ....

Knee-high boots should **never** be too loose in the calf. They are supposed to fit snugly. You don't want them tight, but you also do not want them to sag or slouch unintentionally.

.... ❧[158]❧ ....

Always pick up a can of waterproofing spray in the shoe department. Protect your foul-weather footwear purchase prior to the first wearing. Your rainy-day shoes and snow boots are going to take a beating, so make sure to protect them from the very beginning. There is no reason your winter boots should look worn after one season.

Color

························ ❧[159]❧ ························

Your best colors *always* make you look and feel fantastic because they harmonize with the tones found in your eyes, hair, and skin. When shopping for color, think of yourself as the subject of a portrait. The colors of your clothing, accessories, and makeup are the colors that the artist would use to paint the background and make you come alive. When in doubt on a certain color, look at it in the palm of your hand. Does your skin look more healthy and radiant or less so?

························ ❧[160]❧ ························

Never select a color because it is the color of the moment. Color should always be thought of as a tool, used to showcase you. Just because a color is on trend does not mean you should wear it. If it does not rank an A+ in flattering you, pass it by and shop for one that does.

HOW TO SHOP FOR
a Date

"Don't wear anything you don't feel 100 percent confident in. A date is *not* the time to experiment with a new look! When you're confident, you're relaxed and you're able to chat—to share and to be the best version of yourself. Your outfit should be the last thing on your mind once you leave the house."

—**COCO ROCHA,** *model*

✳ Think about shopping for a first date the same way you would for a portrait. Ask yourself if the picture of you in this outfit captures the most authentic and best version of you at this particular moment of your life.

✳ Most dates are seated over dinner or drinks, so put the emphasis on shopping from the waist up. Look for a flattering neckline that follows the shape of your jaw.

✳ Consider sparkling (literally) by adding some sequins, beads, or embellishment to your look.

✳ Don't shop for a pattern or something with a large logo. The focus should be on you in a solid, beautiful color!

✳ Err on the more formal side when shopping for date clothes. It conveys a feeling that you want to be there and respect the experience and the other person.

✳ Don't buy anything too sexy for a first date.

✳ If you are dating more than one person at once, shopping a duplicate of your absolute favorite "date top" might be a good idea. It will ensure that you feel as vibrant on the Tuesday date as you do on your Wednesday one.

✳ Don't get anything that's overly complicated. Who needs straps falling, ties opening, or billowy sleeves dipping into food when you're trying to get to know someone?

✳ Stay clear of loose-fitting date clothing that you would deem "languid." It may give off a passive vibe, as though you don't want to be on the date, instead of a more energetic "I want to be here" feeling.

✳ Use your favorite lipstick as a color cue for what to wear. It will show your passion and vitality.

✳ A focal point item can start a conversation or function as an icebreaker, so always keep your eye out for the slightly unexpected as you shop!

✳ A date can be a great time to wear sexy shoes. Just make sure you'll be sitting in a restaurant or theater and not hiking or cycling.

················· ❧[161]❧ ·················

Match the lightest or darkest tone of your
eyes to a garment, and you will always seem
friendly and approachable when you wear
it. Eyes have been called the windows to the
soul, and these particular shades ignite them.
Note: Brown eyes are not always brown. While
shopping, try on greens, yellows, purples, and
oranges to help you see beyond the brown and
discover your version of this soothing hue.

················· ❧[162]❧ ·················

When buying a print, always make sure that
about 75 percent of the colors in it are your
most flattering. Designers are not thinking
about your particular color palette. They are
often inspired by how particular colors look
together. Therefore, let majority rule your
shopping choice. Choose your best colors
when completing the outfit with other
clothing and accessories, and ignore the less
flattering ones.

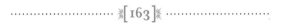

A color that looks great on you will *always* make your skin look more radiant. Hold the compact of your favorite foundation in the palm of your hand and notice how healthy your skin looks against it. When you're out shopping, keep this "glowy" goal in mind. Your rule should be to only purchase the colors that keep your skin looking healthy. Avoid the tones that separate the pigments, or make you think, "Hmm, maybe this would work with slightly different makeup."

Fabrics that are textured or shiny will *always* make you appear larger. Shine will reflect light and give the illusion of larger-than-life. Textured fabrics are not flat to the body and will also give you a larger appearance. Don't be afraid of these items; rather, use them strategically to your advantage.

································· ❧[165]❧ ·······························

Sometimes just because something is in one of your most flattering colors does not mean you should buy it. There are still factors of fit, texture, and styling to consider. The truth is, unless your profession is that of the muse, designers are not designing specifically for you. There may be some seasons when the colors that suit you may not be offered in your best cut, fabric, or style. Don't settle. Everything that you purchase should showcase you at your very best.

····························· ❧[166]❧ ·····························

A neutral will **never** make a greater impression than a flattering color. Each color can be identified with an emotion and a place or period of history, so they always have a specific visual impact. For instance, bright yellow evokes a sunny day. Wedgwood Blue is reminiscent of the eighteenth century. ↳

At the end of the day, neutrals are, well, neutral. The woman in merlot, turquoise, or buttercup is the one who we remember, so if an item is available in both a neutral and a color, go for the latter and make an impression.

························ ❋[167]❋ ························

Shop for a winter coat in a nonneutral as it will **always** brighten up a blustery day— and you'll actually look forward to wearing it! When the temperature goes down, perk yourself up with a healthy dose of color. Think of the sea of gray and black winter coats on a frigid day and the lovely burst of optimism that a jade-colored coat can bring to it. It not only feels great to wear, but also guarantees smiles on the street from those welcoming a momentary distraction from the current temperature.

How to Shop for
Patterns and Prints

"Whether striped, polka-dotted, or floral, a pattern instantly tells us something character-defining about the person who wears it. Embrace the power of pattern and print!"

—**Carol Burnett,** *award-winning actress, comedian, singer, and writer*

✳ The scale of a print should be proportionate to your size.

✳ Don't go for polka dots, flowers, or any other motif that is larger than your palm. You will get lost in it.

✳ Base your purchasing decision on the most dominant color of a pattern and not on the less prominent hues. To determine the dominant color, try squinting and blurring your eyes.

✳ If the pattern on an item is made up of 75 percent of your most flattering colors, consider purchasing it, but never invest in accessories or coordinating items in the less-flattering tones.

✳ If you are experimenting with pattern for the first time, the best first step is to try a tone-on-tone, in a color that always gets you the most compliments.

✳ By going beyond stripes and checks, you may discover that gentler patterns like confetti and watercolor designs connect with your personality better.

⁎ Base the contrast level of a print on your own coloring. Never purchase a muted pattern if you have highly contrasted coloring such as pale skin and dark hair, or a high-contrast print if your personal coloring is more blended.

⁎ The reason a pattern does not quite work might have nothing to do with the colors or design but rather the contrast level. If thoughts of pumping up or blending your makeup enter your mind when you try it on, this is most probably the case.

⁎ Prints or patterns paired with neutrals will always work.

⁎ Don't purchase something in a pattern that at first glance reminds you of any sort of service uniform. You will never want to wear it.

⁎ Shop a micro stripe, plaid, or check to add texture to your wardrobe and ensure that you are wearing a pattern that will not dominate you, no matter how vibrant.

⁎ Don't be afraid to mix prints or patterns. Just make sure they are complementary and choose one print or pattern to be the leader.

⁎ When shopping for patterns to mix together, select smaller ones to wear closest to your face. This will ensure that the head-to-toe combination will never wear you.

⁎ Polka dots and stripes can pair well together.

························· ❧[168]❧ ·························

$\mathcal{N}$ever feel restricted by seasonal colors. Your own personal coloring works year-round, so you should always wear the colors that flatter you. Color should always be thought of as a raw material to enhance you, and the more unexpected, the more exciting. When shopping, keep your personal palette in the forefront and the result will be a wardrobe as unique and singular as you are.

························· ❧[169]❧ ·························

Take advantage of the light and mirrors in the fitting room and determine the color around your iris. It will always be a perfect neutral color. This color already exists in your eye and is part of your natural palette. Potential candidates for this color include olive, chocolate, navy, charcoal, and black.

❧[170]❧

Never discount something in a color that matches your skin tone. This is the softest, most subtle color on your personal palette and should be thought of as your nude. If it is the perfect match, it will be subtle but also illuminating, and will give you a healthy glow! It is sensational in softly textured fabrics like satin and cashmere, and should be worn whenever you want to express your sensuality.

❧[171]❧

Never try to determine a color in person without the influence of some natural light. Store lighting can distort color, and all fabrics catch light differently. To help determine whether or not a color is an A+ one, ask a sales associate where there might be a window as well as a mirror. Only after seeing yourself in natural light should you make the decision to buy or bypass.

Makeup

> "Great makeup keeps a woman looking exactly like herself, only better!"

—**ROBIN KAISER**, *four-time Emmy Award–winning makeup artist*

* If you are attracted to a lipstick color but find that it seems too strong when you try it on, consider the same tone in a translucent gloss.

* You can find a great lipstick color by matching the darkest tone of your flushed skin.

* Shop for an eyeliner that matches the ring around your iris.

* Note the darkest or lightest color from your iris to find an eye shadow that really makes your eyes pop.

* Match the lightest color from your hair for a great neutral eye shadow.

* If your eyes naturally sparkle, consider a satin-finish foundation. If they're tranquil, look at a matte finish.

* It is absolutely okay to ignore one or more of the colors in a multipack eye shadow kit.

* If you like a particular product or color from a certain brand, keep them on your radar by checking in frequently via the Internet or by walking into the store. You share an aesthetic with that brand, and it is possible that there will be other products or colors that please and flatter you!

* Don't dismiss a powder or foundation color just by looking at it in the compact. The color will always appear different when on your skin.

* If you find the perfect product in "your" color, stock up on it since it is likely to be discontinued at some point.

* If you require assistance at the makeup counter, be sure to share with the salesperson the palette of colors you regularly wear.

* When shopping for a new element to add to your current makeup, be sure to wear your usual "face" to the store.

* Don't shop for a new set of makeup to help you coordinate with one particular outfit. It is a clue that the outfit is not the perfect tone for you!

················· ❧[172]❦ ·················

If two different items come in the same color, *always* wait to choose between them until after you have tried both on. It may seem easy to decide which item you prefer just by looking. However, you will absolutely make a more informed decision if you try both pieces on. Remember, the question is how the garment looks on you, not on the shelf.

················· ❧[173]❦ ·················

Never trust that the same item in a different color will fit exactly the same. If you love something in one color, it stands to reason that it'll fit equally well in another. It makes sense, but it doesn't always work out in reality. It is always a good idea to try on every item.

CHAPTER FOUR

DISCOVERING

Hidden Treasures

How to find amazing items at vintage and thrift stores and shop sample sales.

VINTAGE AND THRIFT STORES

·· ⁍[174]⁌ ··

A bit of research online will **always** help you find the best thrift stores, yard sales, estate sales, and antiques malls in your area. Knowledge is power. A bit of it (accessed through some online research), along with the reading of user reviews, will give you valuable insight into your local alternative shopping options. Aimlessly hitting shops and sales that you stumble across will not give you the same success rate as intentionally shopping preselected stores. By researching them carefully, you will also learn what to expect in terms of price points, hours, and the best times to shop.

.... ❧[175]❧ ....

Always figure the cleaning cost into thrift store shopping. You will be happier if your items feel like new! Like anything in your closet, you won't wear something if it is not clean. You have no idea where your thrift shop scores may have been or how dirty (or clean) they might really be, so it is always a great idea to wash or dry-clean them before adding them to your closet. If you are on a tight budget, make sure to check the prices at your local dry cleaner beforehand to avoid any potential surprises.

.... ❧[176]❧ ....

Always hold up items to the light to better find possible imperfections. Just as you should look carefully at the cut, color, and fit of everything you find in a thrift store, you should also be completely clear on the condition. Secondhand items are rarely returnable.

································ ⟫[177]⟪ ································

Never buy anything that is not in great condition. If the garment is telegraphing "old and used," do you really want it to say the same about you and your style? The reality is that repairing an item may cost more than you paid for it. Is it worth it? In most cases, no. The only exception is if you vow to go directly to a tailor or shoe repair shop for mending, or if you yourself are an accomplished seamstress or leathersmith looking for a new project.

································ ⟫[178]⟪ ································

Buttons made of pearl or brass always indicate a quality garment. In this case, the art is in the details. Fine buttons are a clue to fine quality. Pearl and brass buttons are more expensive, and therefore used only by higher-end fashion houses to decorate designer clothing.

························ ❧[179]❧ ························

Poor quality will always be more noticeable on a light-colored item. Just as it is easier to see a stain on something white than on something black, light colors also show their quality more honestly. Darker colors help hide sewing imperfections and less-luxurious fabrics. As a general rule, steer clear of low-quality light colors at the thrift store. Instead, consider darker ones that can be mixed with higher-quality pieces and blended into an effective head-to-toe look.

························ ❧[180]❧ ························

Dress weights are always a sign of good quality. Designer dresses, blouses, and skirts are often weighted with what look like small metal washers. Dress weights are used to stabilize lighter-weight fabrics and keep the shape of a bib or cowl neck detail. They are most frequently found sewn into the hem of a formal skirt or train.

········· ❧[181]❧ ·········

Always consider how something smells when shopping for vintage items. Smells can be very difficult to get out. Some odors can be lessened or eliminated just by airing the garment outside. If the item is washable, there is a good chance of removing a smell completely, even if it requires a second cycle. However, if the label reads "dry clean only," keep in mind that dry cleaning is a waterless process that does not remove odors as thoroughly as regular laundry. Perspiration, smoke, mold, and perfume odors will need special attention. If you have any doubt that the smell will linger even after the expense of cleaning, it is best to leave it on the sales rack.

········· ❧[182]❧ ·········

Keep in mind that a thrift store item made of a natural fiber in a light, unflattering color can **sometimes** be dyed a darker, more flattering tone—but a darker item will never come out in an even hue when using color remover. ↪

Have you discovered something in your best style, but in a color that does nothing for you? Check the tag—the percentage of natural fiber in the garment will determine how much color it will absorb (100 percent cotton, for instance, absorbs color well). Unfortunately, color removal doesn't work the same way. Fabrics will not fade evenly, and variables such as fabric treatment and dry cleaning combined with color remover will often produce streaks and blotches.

·························· ≉[183]≉ ··························

Always check armholes for perspiration marks. No matter how the condition of something appears, flip up the sleeves and check underneath the armholes for pit stains. Perspiration marks are usually permanent, and are not a desirable detail to include in your perfect wardrobe.

············· ≫[184]≪ ·············

If an item shows any sign of possibilities, always grab it and carry it with you as you survey the rest of the store. There is typically only one of each specific item in a secondhand shop, so there is a high probability that more than one person could be interested in purchasing it. Therefore, do not stop at each item that interests you and weigh its pros and cons. Instead, thwart the efforts of your competitors by doing a full sweep of the entire place, pulling out and holding on to all of the things that have potential. Only after you have canvassed the entire store should you begin the try-on and editing process.

············· ≫[185]≪ ·············

Sometimes a thrift store will be understaffed and items discarded at the register may not be immediately restocked. Always ask to peek at the rack of other people's point-of-purchase discards. Because there is typically only one of each particular item, and the potential ↬

of it being snapped up by the competition is always strong, thrift store shopping requires quick decision making. Shoppers often carry around potential purchases and wait to narrow down their choices until they are at the register. Their last-minute edits at the register can become your thrift shop scores! Likewise, when items do make it back to the rack, they may be restocked in completely random sections, so it's worth at least a glance through every section.

·························· ⟨[186]⟩ ··························

There will *always* be one day per week when the largest amount of new items are tagged and ready for sale. By doing some research or simply by asking an employee, you can discover what day the fresh merchandise hits the floor. You might even be able to find out what time it arrives to ensure the greatest variety and increase your chances of finding something perfect. Once you discover the date and time, you should add it as a recurring event in your day planner or calendar.

······················· ❊[187]❊ ·······················

Thrift and consignment shops in a suburb of an affluent city often receive fantastic designer merchandise, always with much milder shopping competition and lower prices than in the city itself. Women with money typically shop and spend more, often at higher-end stores and boutiques. When they weed out their closets, the discards have to end up somewhere, and it is likely that they will land at a consignment or thrift shop not far from where they live. It is definitely worth frequenting these places since many people living in affluent areas do not shop secondhand, making the chances of finding great items at fantastic prices quite high.

······················· ❊[188]❊ ·······················

Never forget to sign up for email notifications and special promotions at thrift and consignment stores. Sign up and you will be notified not only about regular discount days and events but also end-of-season ↪

blowouts that you will not want to miss, including twice-yearly fill-a-bag sales. Just as regular-priced stores hustle the remnants of last season out the door with deep discounts, secondhand stores often follow suit by offering a bag at the door for a set price that you are welcome to fill with whatever fits inside. Make sure to arrive early, as these tend to be *very* popular shopping events!

[189]

The most interesting closets are those that include some variety, and you will always add variety to your wardrobe by introducing the style and aesthetic of another geographic region. Shopping in your home area may offer you only the choices or "look" of that particular region, be it preppy, beachy, and so on. When you travel, research thrift and consignment shops en route to or near your destination to spice up your wardrobe with some new regional flavors.

··· ❧[190]❧ ···

Thrift and consignment stores often offer discounts to senior citizens, so **always** think about incorporating a shopping trip into your next lunch date with Grandma. Seniors can save between 15 and 50 percent on their purchases, but there may be restrictions. This discount is occasionally extended to those aged fifty-five and up, but is more commonly reserved for shoppers who are at least sixty-two or sixty-five years old. It is sometimes reserved for one particular day of the week, with Wednesday being a common choice. This deal may not be advertised, so check ahead, and do not be shy about asking for it at the register. Also, remind your grandmother to bring her ID with her in case she needs to prove she is older than she looks.

SAMPLE SALES

················· ⚜[191]⚜ ·················

Always check out the payment options prior to your arrival at a sample sale. Designer sample sales are often specific about which credit cards they accept. Some are cash only. You don't want to get caught without any way to pay.

················· ⚜[192]⚜ ·················

Never arrive less than two hours ahead. There will most likely be a line. The most eager shoppers will grab the best stuff right away.

················· ⚜[193]⚜ ·················

Sometimes a designer sample sale is not *really* a sample sale. A true designer sample sale will feature merchandise in a size 2 or 4. An *overstock sale* may feature an array of sizes.

SHOPPING FOR
Your Wedding

"To create the most memorable wedding, incorporate meaningful personal touches inspired by the couple's lives and the unique cultures and traditions of their families."

—**MARA URSHEL**, *co-owner, Kleinfeld*

✳ Start your shopping twelve months prior to the big day. The average lead time to receive a wedding gown that has been ordered is between five and eight months.

✳ Shop for a wedding gown in December. New gowns arrive throughout November, so everything should be in stock.

✳ Don't shop for a wedding dress before knowing what time of year and time of day you are planning the ceremony.

✳ Your wedding is as unique as you are. Don't feel compelled to shop for a dress or accessories that echo what your mother, sister, or best friend wore.

✳ Keep in mind that the more people you bring along for your wedding dress shopping, the more conflicting tastes and opinions you will get!

✳ Trying on too many wedding dresses only leads to confusion. Arrive for your first dress fitting with the intention of only trying on your top five favorite dresses.

* Don't try on wedding gowns that are more than 10 percent above your maximum budget. There is a chance you will fall in love with the unobtainable, and all others going forward in your search will pale in comparison.

* Don't try on dresses without the proper foundation garments and the exact heel height you plan to wear.

* Reference the white of your eye to find the most complementary shade of white to wear for your wedding day.

* Look for clues in your closet as to the style, neckline, and fabric of what will be your most flattering wedding gown.

* The wedding dress that you admire on someone else or on a hanger may not translate or capture the same thing on you. Don't think twice about scrapping the idea and going in another direction.

* If you know the style, size, and fit you are looking for, looking at secondhand dresses found online from independent sellers can be a great low-cost option.

* Though many brides lose weight in anticipation of their big day, you should always order your dress in your current size. It is easier and less expensive to take a dress in and will lessen the pressure.

* Remember to budget for dress alterations, which may be more than you have spent on any other tailoring.

continued

✳ You can save money on shopping by incorporating the "something borrowed" idea. Flatter a friend or relative by asking to wear a piece of her jewelry on the big day.

✳ Don't give your attendants the job of shopping for their own dresses without giving them very specific information on the cut, length, and color scheme you envision.

✳ Looking to the blue, green, or purple of the vein color in your wrist will give you the absolutely perfect color choice for your bridesmaids' dresses.

✳ Purchasing a tuxedo or suit may be much more economical than renting one. Once bought, it can be used again.

✳ When shopping for a bouquet, work with your florist to ensure that the scale is right by requesting that no one flower is more than half the size of your hand.

❧[194]❧

Always try to get a preview of a designer sample sale by checking out specialty blogs to see if the merchandise and price points are "you." Not all sample sales are for everyone; only go to the ones where you will likely make a purchase. A quick check online can save you time and energy.

❧[195]❧

Always be prepared to change in front of people when shopping a sample sale. Sample sales do not happen in stores with dressing rooms. There may be a corner you can change in or a screen you can change behind, but it's worth it to assume you will be changing in front of other people—wear tights or a camisole if you are shy.

·········· 〚196〛 ··········

Always wear thin, body-conscious layers to a sample sale. As there will not likely be a dressing room, wearing layers is a great way to dress. You can peel them away to suit what you're trying on.

·········· 〚197〛 ··········

Sample sales are *always* crowded during lunch (11:30 a.m. to 2 p.m.). Many people will only be able to attend during their lunch hour. If you can avoid going during this time, you will find the sale less crowded. If you can get there before lunch, there will be much more merchandise available.

·········· 〚198〛 ··········

You are *never* obligated to buy anything, even if the designer is there. It can be awkward if the designer is present, but if you are not in love with an item, resist the feeling that you need to buy something in order to avoid insulting ↪

him or her. If pressed, you can simply say you need a bit of time to think about it.

.... ❊[199]❊ ....

Sometimes you can negotiate the price of a piece if it is missing a button or has a broken zipper. Garments are not always in perfect condition at a sample sale. That is okay; it can work to your advantage. Ask for a discount if you notice an imperfection.

.... ❊[200]❊ ....

Dividing and conquering with a friend who knows your sizes and color palette will always help maximize your success rate. If you two make a plan to look for each other as you look for yourselves, you'll have double the chance of finding a treasure.

········· ❧[201]❧ ·········

$\mathscr{A}$lways keep an eye on your potential purchases. With people changing in a shared area, it can be easy for someone to accidentally grab someone else's shopping stash. Most important, keep in mind that your personal belongings can be mistaken for merchandise.

········· ❧[202]❧ ·········

$\mathscr{N}$ever get caught up in sample sale fever. Even after waiting on line for hours, if what you see is not as great as what is in your closet, move on!

CHAPTER FIVE

MASTERING

the Virtual Store

Your tutorial
on online shopping.

.... ❋[203]❋ ....

*A*lways send those too-frequent emails from your favorite stores directly to your spam folder. This way you can review them weekly and stay informed without being overwhelmed. If you see these emails too often, it is likely you will become annoyed and may unsubscribe, thus missing out on future savings.

.... ❋[204]❋ ....

*A*lways shop at reputable websites. The web address of the page you enter your credit card information on should begin with *https,* not just *http.* This ensures it is safe and secure.

[205]

Never shop on a public computer or when using a public Wi-Fi network. You don't want to take any chances on anyone having access to your credit card information. It's completely safe to browse under these circumstances, but never enter any personal information.

[206]

If you're buying directly from an individual seller online, always check the customer feedback. There are so many great sellers out there, and most people are honest. But unfortunately you will also find enough scams to make you wary. Checking a seller's feedback is a great way to learn if other people have had a bad experience. Chances are, if someone has been honest in the past, she's not going to start cheating people now.

·············· ❧[207]❦ ··············

Always make use of the online sizing charts. The most obvious downside of online shopping is that you can't try anything on. However, almost all online stores have sizing charts. Always consult these charts, as sizes can vary from line to line. Some websites even have stylists you can email with questions. This service is invaluable, because they can tell you if a brand runs big or small or true to size.

·············· ❧[208]❦ ··············

Never buy anything online without first checking the return and delivery policies. To avoid getting stuck with an unwanted purchase, make sure you check the site's return policy. You also want to check the delivery policy and make sure your item will arrive with enough time to return if necessary. If you can't find the policies on the website, email customer service for that information.

.... ❊[209]❊ ....

When shopping online, *always* narrow your search by entering your size and budget info. Searching for an item can be overwhelming and time consuming. It's no fun to scroll through page after page of items you're not interested in. If you enter your size and price range, you will cut down on the number of displayed items significantly.

.... ❊[210]❊ ....

Never trust a color name when shopping on the Internet. The description—and even the visual—may be inaccurate. Go by what the color looks like to you and, if possible, look at it on two different devices to discern the shade.

.... ❊[211]❊ ....

When unsure about a fabric, *always* use the zoom feature. Sites will always list the fabric of a garment, but if you're not familiar with it, zoom in. You will see subtleties such as texture and sheen that you may otherwise miss.

.... ⟩[212]⟨ ....

Never buy a garment online unless it is shown somewhere on a model. It may seem picky, but seeing a flat picture of a piece of clothing means you're only getting half of the information. You need to see how it hangs on the body to really get a feel for the garment.

.... ⟩[213]⟨ ....

Always read online reviews of products in question. Reading other customer's reviews can answer many of your questions. It can also save you the trouble of having to send something back due to fit, color, or quality.

.... ⟩[214]⟨ ....

If you're unsure of an item, always add it to your online cart. This will give you time to think about it, and when you come back to the site, it'll be there and you won't lose your time and patience looking for it again.

.... ⟩[215]⟨ ....

Sometimes, if you place an item in your online shopping cart and close the browser window without buying, you will receive a discount promo code from the retailer within forty-eight hours in an attempt to sway you to complete your purchase. Don't let this lure you into buying something you are unsure of. However, if you do really want the item, use it to your advantage!

.... ⟩[216]⟨ ....

Always feel free to communicate with online customer service. They are your best asset when shopping online. Customer service can answer almost anything, and can tell you when an item will be marked down.

.... ⟩[217]⟨ ....

Always shop online on Tuesdays. While it can be tempting to shop online any day of the week, you're better off waiting until Tuesday. It's the day most sites post sales and new items.

HOW TO SHOP FOR
Glasses

"Don't follow fashion, follow the contours of your face. Also, for the record—wearing glasses *does* make you more intelligent. In my case, they enable me to read!"

—**SIMON COLLINS**, *Former Dean of Fashion, Parsons The New School for Design*

* Wear your contacts when shopping for frames so you can see what they look like both close up and far away.

* If you wear eyeglasses all the time, think of them as an accessory that you need to coordinate with each and every item that you wear.

* Follow the shape of your brow in determining and shopping the best frame shape for your face.

* If you expect to wear your glasses most of the time, think about shopping frames that are light on the face, such as clear, metallic, or rimless pairs.

* The arms of your glasses should never be too loose or too tight.

* When choosing a color for eyeglasses, match a color found in your eyes or hair, or take a cue from the color of your favorite jewelry metal.

✳ If you do not always want your glasses to be a strong element in your head-to-toe look, make them recede and go for rimless or half-rim glasses.

✳ Take advantage of "Buy One, Get One Half Off" eyeglasses promotions. It is a great idea to have a second style to both add variety to your wardrobe and have as a backup.

✳ A second pair of glasses can be your "weekend" or "fun" glasses, so feel free to go wilder in color or shape.

✳ If you only occasionally wear glasses, think about shopping something that's more of a focal point, such as a retro style or something in one of your best, most vibrant colors.

✳ When purchasing glasses, ask for a cloth or wipes at the optometrist's or optician's office to ensure you have them when needed.

✳ When choosing a pair of sunglasses, go more "statement" and take a cue from your favorite era for inspiration!

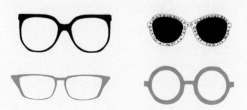

.... ❧[218]❧ ....

Always designate one credit card for all of your online shopping. This makes it easier to track charges as well as return credits.

.... ❧[219]❧ ....

Online coupon codes are *always* initiated at the beginning or end of a month. Seek out a coupon code by searching online to see if one is available for you to use.

.... ❧[220]❧ ....

Always compare prices. Finding a coveted item online can be exciting, but resist the urge to buy until you have compared prices on several sites. You may be surprised to find that different sites can offer the same exact item at different prices. However, keep in mind that you only want to make your purchase on a reputable site.

·························· ❧[221]❧ ··························

*A*lways shop online flash sales early. Things go fast at a flash sale, so make sure you get there at the beginning.

·························· ❧[222]❧ ··························

To get a fab shoe that's guaranteed to fit from an online flash sale, *always* order two sizes with the intention of returning one. Shoe sizes vary from brand to brand. If you get your size, plus a second bigger or smaller pair, you'll have the best shot at getting the right fit.

·························· ❧[223]❧ ··························

*N*ever buy something on the Internet that can't be returned. No matter how good a deal you get or how hard to find something may be, don't ever buy any item you can't send back. There is always the possibility of fraud, so why take a chance? Any reputable seller should be willing to accept a return.

HOW TO SHOP FOR
Your Pregnancy

"Show it off! Your pregnancy is a great time to channel your inner fashionista, and be fabulous. Celebrate, shop, and show off that bump!" —ANA ORTIZ, *actress*

* As you are shopping a temporary wardrobe while pregnant, buying fewer clothes in a tight palette of your very best neutrals will enable you to save money. Neutrals will easily mix and match, and you can add some pop with a colorful accessory or handbag.

* Style your bump as if it were an accessory.

* Early into your first trimester, invest in a belly band. It not only provides back support but can save you money, extending the lifespan of your pre-pregnancy clothing by smoothing out your midsection.

* Shop new bras and extenders at the top of the second trimester, and show off your bump in everything and anything made of jersey.

* Balance your bump in the third trimester. Turn your shopping eye toward bigger and bolder jewelry, scarves, and handbags.

* Shop anything that wraps as it will be useful,

no matter how your body changes. It can be tied or wrapped looser or tighter depending on how your pregnant body expands.

* Splurge on your accessories while pregnant. Jewelry, scarves, and handbags will work at any trimester, and even after the baby arrives.

* Your head-to-toe look may be more effective if you shop one fewer element of each outfit than you would have pre-pregnancy.

* Shopping for your maternity clothes at a lower price point than your non-maternity wardrobe may give you a larger variety of styles, shapes, and sizes to dress your constantly changing body.

* As your senses are heightened during pregnancy, think about fabric care while shopping. An item in your closet with a strong dry-cleaning smell may end up being passed over and never worn.

* Feet swell during pregnancy, so think about shopping for shoes with good arch support in a breathable material one half-size larger than your pre-maternity size. Avoid lace-ups, since bending over to tie them with an expanded belly can be difficult.

* Wait to shop for post-pregnancy clothes. A woman's body changes after having a baby, and your pre-pregnancy body may not be the exact same as your post-pregnancy one.

* Losing weight after the baby arrives is gradual. To save shopping time in-store and prevent returns online, check your closet to determine what your current size is.

·· ❧[224]❦ ··

Always double-check your online purchase before submitting the order, and never click on it twice. Check that you clicked on the correct item and entered the right quantity. If you're unsure whether or not your order has gone through, *do not* click again. Wait to see if you get a confirmation email and if you don't, call or email customer service to make sure that your order went through.

·· ❧[225]❦ ··

Websites will **sometimes** offer a discount for first-time shoppers. They want you as a customer, and this is their way to entice you. You should absolutely take advantage of this if you were going to buy from the site anyway. If it is not listed, never be afraid to email customer service and ask for a discount. Okay, we admit this next part may be considered shady, but if you have already shopped the site and need the discount in order for something to be in your budget, log out and shop with ↪

a new profile created with a secondary email address. The retailer will not suffer and will be happy for your purchase.

························· ❊[226]❊ ·························

Always say "yes" to registering on an online site. You will then be put on a list for special deals and discounts going forward. You can always have a secondary email address devoted to these sites, which will prevent their promotional emails from going to your day-to-day in-box. Then, when you're ready, you'll have numerous deals and coupons waiting for you.

························· ❊[227]❊ ·························

When shopping online, *always* hold on to the original shipping box until you are certain you are happy with your purchase. It's bad enough if you're unhappy with your purchase and have to send it back. Why add to that by having to go and find the right size box to ship it back in?

·········· ❧[228]❧ ··········

 $\mathscr{N}$ever delete your confirmation email until you are certain you won't need to make a return. This email will have all the necessary information for a return or exchange. Start a folder to file confirmation emails as a way to track what you've bought over a period of time.

CHAPTER SIX

THE

OF THE DEAL

The ins and outs
of getting the best
possible discount.

Always arrive early to a sale, as things may go quickly. The old saying "The early bird catches the worm" could not be more true than when applied to a sale. Retailers are determined to make room for new merchandise (which might already be on their loading dock) by getting the current sale merchandise out the door. Typically nothing will be held back. With all items and sizes on the selling floor, they can go quickly. If you have been eyeing a must-have item at full price all season, set your alarm clock and get to the sale bright and early!

······················ ※[230]※ ······················

𝒜lways ask for a discount before you pay full
price. It seems crazy to think that it's possible
to negotiate the price of something in a store.
It's not a flea market! But the truth is, you
absolutely can. Ask to speak with the manager
and see if you can get a discount. The worst
that can happen is they say no, but in many
cases you can get 10 percent off.

······················ ※[231]※ ······················

𝒩ever buy something just because it's
discounted. You get much more of a rush
finding the perfect piece at a discount than at
full price. However, many of us can fall victim
to "sale fever." We get caught up in the moment
and the thought of the money we are saving
on a not-so-perfect item. The result can be
that very item hanging in your closet unworn
with the tags still on one year later. Although a
piece may be beautiful and can be purchased
at a steal, if it is not an A+ piece on *you*, it has
zero value to your wardrobe!

························· ❊[232]❊ ·························

You can **sometimes** save extra money by
shopping at the end of a sale. Waiting until
the last day of a sale might mean you risk
missing out on some fantastic things in your
size, but it might be worth it for the substantial
final discounts. If a store has quite a bit of
merchandise left at the end of the season,
there will often be a final, additional discount
to liquidate it. The retailer would much rather
sell it to you in-store than have to pay to
inventory and transport it to another location,
such as an outlet.

························· ❊[233]❊ ·························

A sale is **never** really a sale unless you're
getting at least 30 percent off. The word
"sale" is often used when the terms "courtesy
discount" or "promotional price" are more
accurate. If you are only interested in shopping
items that are substantially discounted, read
sale ads and emails carefully to determine the
exact percentage off *before* heading to the ↪

store or adding the opening time of a flash sale to your calendar. Then decide whether the sale is worth your time.

········· ⟩[234]⟨ ·········

Sometimes if you buy something that has since gone on sale, the store will credit the difference. Keep a receipt envelope in a pocket of your purse. After a purchase, place the receipt inside the envelope and keep it there for thirty days. If you happen to be in a store that you recently shopped in and notice a previously purchased item on sale, show your receipt to a sales associate and inquire whether you can get a refund on the difference.

········· ⟩[235]⟨ ·········

Sale merchandise is **sometimes** purposefully disorganized. It doesn't seem to make sense that a store would want a messy rack or shelf. However, they may do this so that in your frustration you will resist the chaos and reach for full-price items instead.

················· ❊[236]❊ ·····················

$\mathcal{N}$ever be fooled by a "Buy One, Get One"
discount. The point is to get you to spend more
money. A discount on two of the same item
is only a good deal if you actually need two.
Exceptions to this would be if it is the perfect
basic piece for your wardrobe or if it functions
as part of a work uniform. In either case,
having two will ensure that you will always
have a clean one to wear. A third exception is if
you plan to keep one item for yourself and give
the other as a gift.

················· ❊[237]❊ ·····················

An item will almost always go on sale after six
to eight weeks. If there's something you covet,
keep an eye on it, and you might end up getting
it for less. Fashion moves briskly. It's all about
providing a steady stream of new merchandise
for the customer to buy. Statistics on today's
retail marketplace show that at least 40 percent
of a store's merchandise will be sold on sale.
Make sure you are there to reap that benefit!

·········· ❧[238]❧ ··········

You can **sometimes** save money by buying the
clothes off the mannequin's back. If the store is
out of stock but a mannequin is wearing what
you want in your size, ask the manager if you
can purchase the display item. Just remember
to check the tag. It may be a bigger size than
it appears, as items are often pinned to fit the
mannequin. Be sure to ask for a discount since
it was the display piece.

·········· ❧[239]❧ ··········

When shopping sale racks, **always** check
the sections to the right and left of your size.
Items frequently get mixed up and your great
find may be hiding! The sale rack is pawed
through countless times each day by shoppers.
Often they will grab many items as potential
purchases, then look at them more carefully
and discard a few. These discards do not always
end up in exactly the right place. Expand your
focus and you may discover the item, size, and
price that are absolutely perfect!

············· ❧[240]❧ ·············

The final sale rack is **always** the perfect place to find the more unusual colors and styles that you look so great in. Basic items in classic neutral colors rarely make it to the end of the season. What do are the more unusual ones. These are the items deemed *window dressing*, which are often used at the front of a department or in a store window to lure the customer to come inside. While drawn in by these attention-grabbing pieces, most shoppers settle on more versatile items, leaving behind some of the most interesting colors and styles—which often end up on sale for a substantial discount.

············· ❧[241]❧ ·············

Always do an online search for promotional codes. Whether shopping online or in-store, retailer-issued promotional codes (also known as coupon or discount codes) can save you money. They may be specific to a certain deal, ↝

offer something such as free shipping, or give you a discount of a set dollar amount or percentage off your total purchase.

·········· ❄[242]❄ ··········

The best clearance sales are always in January and May. Fall and spring are major fashion seasons, when stores purchase a significant amount of merchandise. If full-price retail sales are not strong during these periods, stores have a tremendous amount of items to get rid of to make room for the upcoming season's goods. May, at the end of spring, becomes a logical clearance sale period. Fall merchandise sales are held in January, when all of the remaining stock not sold during the December holidays is liquidated. Fantastic deals can be had by those who do not mind shopping and then putting their purchases away to enjoy next year.

Jewelry

"Accessories are the most important element of fashion. They tell people something about you, and allow 'access' to your personality. They're how you make a look individual and special."

—**FERN MALLIS**, *creator, New York Fashion Week and the FERN FINDS: collection*

✳ Jewelry is a fantastic way to take a risk. You may not like to wear bold prints or shapes, but a great piece of statement jewelry can make the same impression.

✳ If you don't wear crewnecks, don't shop a necklace that is shorter than 18 inches in length. It will create the same unfavorable neckline.

✳ A traditional-style necklace or bracelet receives an instant update

when you shop and layer a second piece in a similar metallic.

✳ If you have a large bust, it may be best to avoid necklaces that hit right at the chest.

✳ If shopping for a necklace that sits above your collarbone, first measure the base of your neck. Then add between two and four inches to ensure the perfect length.

✳ A difficult clasp on the "perfect" necklace or

bracelet may very well become the reason you never wear it, so before you commit factor in the cost and effort of replacing it with a user-friendly one.

✳ When shopping for a ring, think about which hand you are going to wear it on; a finger on your dominant hand can be one half-size larger.

✳ If you are married, never forget that your wedding and engagement rings will always be part of your everyday ensemble, so use their metals, stones, and shapes as a reference to coordinate a head-to-toe look.

✳ It is best to shop for simple earrings along with a focal point necklace. This will ensure that the pieces complement and balance each other. The reverse is true when shopping for focal-point earrings.

✳ When layering bracelets, rings, or necklaces, shop for uneven numbers. This will create a look that is more interesting and fashion forward.

✳ Don't be afraid to mix metals. An exclusive style alliance with silver *or* gold is no longer standard.

···················· ❊[243]❊ ····················

Friday is always the most popular day for
a brick-and-mortar sale to begin. Though
most women shop in the middle of the week,
retailers have figured out that once they're
finished concentrating on their Monday-to-
Friday obligations, they can be swayed to shop
on a weekend with the incentive of a sale.
Therefore, in-store sales are often jump-started
at the top of the weekend.

···················· ❊[244]❊ ····················

Sometimes stores will increase their prices
on a tax-free day. Some U.S. states allow tax-
free shopping on specific days of the year.
Many retailers lower their prices on these
days, as well as offer special sales to bring in
customers. It is a rare occurrence, but there
have been some less reputable retailers who
have actually raised their prices in anticipation
of such days, meaning that you actually end
up spending more than on a regular day. ↪

Check prices before your tax-free shopping trip to guarantee that you are paying the correct ones.

·························· ❧[245]❧ ··························

Shopping a presale event will *always* ensure the best selection of merchandise. If you don't need the instant gratification of carrying a shopping bag out the door, a presale event is a great way to get the items you want at a discounted price. A presale event is a private sale that happens right before an official sale starts. It is advertised quietly, so ask the salespeople at your favorite stores how you can get on the notification list. The way it works is that you make your selections and a salesperson will hold them, along with your credit card information. Once the sale officially begins, your card is charged, and you can then pick up your purchases (or have them sent directly to you, if it's more convenient).

·························· ❧[246]❧ ··························

A sale is *always* a great time to get items in luxury fabrics like silk, cashmere, or other gorgeous fabrics, which at full price can often be out of reach. Make sure, however, that you carefully inspect the condition of each item. Caressable fine fabrics are very delicate, and shoppers have a tendency to touch them in-store, so the possibility of getting a shopworn item is high.

·························· ❧[247]❧ ··························

Sometimes driving to another state to shop will justify the tax savings. If you plan to do more extensive shopping, a map could be just the thing to help stretch your dollars. If your county is not tax free, search for ones nearby that might be, or see if they're having an upcoming tax-free day. Also, if you plan on taking a vacation or business trip, check the tax status and shopping options in the area you are visiting, as well as those you may be traveling through.

CHAPTER SEVEN

When and How to

Splurge

Learn how to indulge your caviar dreams and say "yes" to luxury.

·········· ❧[248]❧ ··········

You may **sometimes** splurge on an item you adore, but make sure it's wearable. If you have a bit of extra money and come across something you absolutely love, go for it. If it's something you can wear for years to come, it's a great investment. However, nothing is worth a lot of money if you're not going to wear it.

·········· ❧[249]❧ ··········

It is **never** okay to spend more than you can comfortably afford on a luxury item. Avoid the temptation of shopping beyond your means, or anxiety will soon become your go-to accessory. Resist torturing yourself by looking at and ↪

trying on out-of-budget items. Instead, determine your price ceiling for a luxury item and stick to it. Visit the stores and departments whose price points are in step with yours, and always set your spending limit when searching a website or flash sale.

················· ❊[250]❊ ·················

Never splurge on a trend. That must-have piece is likely to be passé before you're done paying it off. Trends are, well, trends—here today and gone tomorrow. The great thing about them is that when they hit, they hit at every price point. Therefore, think about buying your trendiest pieces at lower price points to ensure that you feel no remorse next season when fashion moves forward.

⋙[251]⋘

Invest in a timeless quality piece. A timeless item is always in fashion, no matter what is happening in current trends. If you need help determining which types of pieces would fall into this category, here's an exercise: Take a look at photos of yourself from the time you entered adulthood until today. When analyzing each head-to-toe look, notice which clothes and accessories stay completely classic and do not define a particular time or place. These are your timeless pieces.

⋙[252]⋘

Sometimes the most expensive item in your wardrobe, and the one that creates the greatest impact, is an accessory. It can be the special thing that ignites and pulls together a head-to-toe look. Ignore any preconceived rules about spending allotted amounts on particular categories of your closet and spend a little ↝

extra on that piece of jewelry you're confident
will go with almost everything you own.
You know it is perfect when you use
it often, or even daily, to transform
the most basic outfits from
average to extraordinary.

······················· ⟫[253]⟪ ·······················

A "splurge" can always be justified by its
number of wearings—and when you have
something beautiful and of good quality in
your wardrobe, you will be more likely to wear
it often. A great coat, for instance, is a valuable
item to spend more on, since it will not only
be the item that gets the most wear during the
cold and rainy seasons, but it may also last for
many years to come!

························· ❧[254]❧ ·························

A good cashmere sweater is **sometimes** worth splurging on. Cashmere is made in a number of qualities. The better the quality, the longer it will last. In the end, it may be less expensive to purchase one good-quality sweater rather than a succession of lesser-quality ones with shorter shelf lives. To make sure that you get the maximum value out of your sweater, avoid trendy styling and opt for simple, timeless style.

························· ❧[255]❧ ·························

A good-quality wide or skinny belt in your best neutral or metal is **always** a great go-to, all-season item. A belt can be used all year, quickly justifying its price tag. It can be used to perk up and punctuate a pair of pants, a dress, a blouse, or even a coat. If you would like to minimize your waist, take a cue from the dominant neutral color in your closet and find a matching belt; to accentuate your waist, use the predominant metal from your jewelry box.

·········· ⁂[256]⁂ ··········

A hoop earring in a shape that follows your features is **always** the perfect piece to have in your jewelry box. If your features are rounded, repeat them in a round earring. Copy an oval chin in a hoop of the same shape, and choose a triangular or geometric shape to complement more angular features.

·········· ⁂[257]⁂ ··········

A sleek, high-quality handbag that matches the darkest color found in your hair will **always** be timeless and versatile enough to go from day to evening. Keep it sleek without embellishment and hardware.

·························· ❊[258]❊ ··························

It is **sometimes** more interesting to mix formal luxury items with more casual inexpensive pieces. Unless you are one of the rare people who purchase entire looks off of mannequins or pages of magazines, you probably want to put your own stamp on your style. The best and most interesting way to do this is by creating a mix of formal and informal items. For instance, a string of pearls can add polish and sophistication to a T-shirt.

·························· ❊[259]❊ ··························

A splurge is **never** a splurge if it is worn often enough to justify its price tag. Think about how many times you might wear the item in question, and divide its cost among them. Is it justified? Or, if you have ever owned a similar item, how much use did you get out of it? How often was it worn? Weekly? Daily? The answers to these questions will help you discern whether your splurge is indeed a splurge, and whether or not to proceed with your purchase.

HOW TO SHOP FOR
a Purse

"Remember that versatile does not have to mean boring! Finding a color and texture that you love will make you most likely to reach for it again and again."

—LAUREN GOLDBERG, *founder and CEO, Lauren Merkin Handbags*

✳ Put your thumbs together and spread your hands wide for a fail-safe clutch height and width.

✳ Your best clutch should follow the shape of your jaw: angular, square, rounded, or oval.

✳ Take a cue from the metal you wear the most when considering hardware on a purse.

✳ Match your go-to, everyday purse to the darkest color in your hair (see page 155), but don't go for the obvious. Might your brown hair have aubergine or olive in it?

✳ When you put a bag on your shoulder, consider if the logo is more prominent than you are.

✳ When dressing up, remember that the more structured the bag, the more formal it appears.

✳ Look at the texture of your hair to determine whether the material of your purse should be shiny or matte.

✳ Matching the color of a purse to a shoe is fine, but vary the textures.

✳ A pattern on a purse is a great way to tie colors of an outfit together.

························ ❧[260]❧ ························

Fine perfumes are made with higher quality ingredients that may allow you to do more with less. Sometimes the price tag on an expensive fragrance can be justified if you think of it as *the* perfect accessory that will personalize everything you wear! To make a spritz last even longer, apply it immediately after bathing—and get more for your money by requesting a complimentary sample size at the point of purchase.

························ ❧[261]❧ ························

A gift will always go from ordinary to extraordinary when it is monogrammed or engraved with the receiver's initials.

CHAPTER EIGHT

SHOPPING
FOR ALL
Seasons
(AND PEOPLE)

Tips for helping you and your loved ones look great all year.

.... ⟩[262]⟨ ....

You can always pay less if you shop at the end of the season. No need to rush to the store the moment new items arrive. Since merchandise comes in early, your items will still be of the moment if you shop at the end of the season.

.... ⟩[263]⟨ ....

Off-season means off-price at an outlet, so always be open to purchasing a winter coat in July and a bikini in January. So what if you have to wait a bit to wear something if you can get it at a great price? It is worthwhile to take advantage of off-season shopping. And remember, it'll give you more time to shop around for your great find!

·························· ❧[264]❧ ··························

When budgeting for a seasonal wardrobe shopping trip, using the spending ratio of 75 percent on classic items and 25 percent on trendy pieces can **sometimes** keep you focused on things you can wear often and in different ways. Seasonal shopping (and also shopping for a trip) needs to be budgeted so that you have enough variety. By sticking to mostly classics, you will get much more use out of your trendy items.

·························· ❧[265]❧ ··························

Never purchase a seasonal item that does not coordinate with anything currently in your closet. You obviously have limited time to wear clothes that are seasonal. Make it a point to get things you can wear right away, unless you have ample time and energy to find all of the coordinating elements.

Dates
TO REMEMBER

* Fall Contemporary merchandise is **ALWAYS** fully in-store and on the selling floor by July 15.

* Fall Designer merchandise is **ALWAYS** fully in-store and on the selling floor by August 30.

* Spring Contemporary merchandise is **ALWAYS** fully in-store and on the selling floor by January 15.

* Spring Designer merchandise is **ALWAYS** fully in-store and on the selling floor by February 28.

.... ❊[266]❊ ....

$\mathcal{N}$ever buy a swimsuit without trying it on. It can be tricky to find a swimsuit that fits just right. You really need to try on a lot of suits to find your match. Don't just find your size and head to the register. Never try on a suit that doesn't have a covering on the crotch—and never try on a swimsuit without underwear. When you do buy a suit, it's a good idea to wash it before you wear it.

.... ⟩[267]⟨ ....

Always create a collage or online inspiration board prior to major seasonal shopping so you know what it is you are looking for. By pulling up these pictures before you set out, you will be a more focused and efficient shopper.

.... ⟩[268]⟨ ....

Never compromise on support in a swimsuit. If you have more than a B cup (without help from a plastic surgeon), you need support. Take our advice, otherwise your day at the beach will be spent arranging your boobs every twenty minutes.

.... ⟩[269]⟨ ....

You will **sometimes** need to go up a size or two in a swimsuit. It is very common for swimsuits to run small. Don't be alarmed if you need to go up one or more sizes.

.... ※[270]※ ....

A black swimsuit will **always** be slimming. For extra skinniness, try a suit made by a shapewear company.

.... ※[271]※ ....

Never rule out shopping for a light jacket, sweater, or pashmina in the summer. Most people are in air conditioning much of the time and need some coverage. You can also get a great deal at that time of year.

.... ※[272]※ ....

Always wear something on the bulky side when trying on winter coats. This is your protection against spending a winter with sleeves that are too tight, or a coat that won't close properly. You should have plenty of room in your coat, without getting lost in it.

·················· ⟩[273]⟨ ··················

Always get the best coat you can afford. There is no other garment you will be seen in more during the winter. Invest in the best quality without overspending.

·················· ⟩[274]⟨ ··················

It is always a good idea to have a wardrobe of coats if you have a cold-weather winter. Since you are in your coat for so much of the time, it's great to have options. It's okay to wear the same coat every day, but it can be more fun to switch it up.

·················· ⟩[275]⟨ ··················

Always shop for warmth in a winter coat. So many of us shop for a coat before it's actually cold out. Therefore, it can be easy to forget that the main job of the coat is to keep you warm. There are enough stylish options out there that you never have to sacrifice warmth.

·················· ≯[276]≮ ··················

Always think twice about shopping in April. Retailers are counting on your feeling flush after a tax refund and are never as liberal with discounts and sales during that time. Remember: A tax refund is not a gift or found money. It is part of your earnings.

·················· ≯[277]≮ ··················

Swimwear *always* goes on sale in June. Summer is short in most regions, so retailers have a narrow window to sell swimwear, with 60 percent of it sold between May and July. May has become the preview month for the sale-inspired customer who's willing to wait, and the selling month for the fall-in-love-with-it-they-have-my-size-and-pay-full-price customer. June, in the midst of the strongest selling period, has become the time to excite the customer who would love a new suit but would love it more on sale. It's also the time when stores want to start thinning out their stock, with the goal of clearing it all out by August.

························ ※[278]※ ························

October is **never** a great month for a deal. After the back-to-school sales and before the holiday shopping begins is not a good time for getting a discount. Only shop for things you absolutely need in October, and wait another month to indulge without paying full price.

························ ※[279]※ ························

Anything velvet will **always** be on sale by November 15. Velvet is mostly associated with the fall and winter holidays, so if it is not purchased in time for Thanksgiving, it may not sell at all. Its short retail shelf life can be thought of as the cold-weather equivalent of swimwear. Also, velvet does not hold up well on crowded end-of-season sale racks. The delicate fabric is easily dented with permanent hanger marks. It needs to sell while it's still in pristine condition.

································· ⚡[280]⚡ ·····························

Holiday dresses are always in-store no later
than October 30. The holiday selling period
is a short but very important one. So, just as
holiday decorations often go up long before
Halloween to get us into the holiday spirit,
retailers like to get items in-store and online
early in order to excite us—as well as stretch
their selling season and increase the possibility
of sellouts and reorders.

································· ⚡[281]⚡ ·····························

Always shop for Christmas gifts online
during the week of Thanksgiving. Many
sites have sales leading up to the day after
Thanksgiving, more commonly known as Black
Friday. The digital version of Black Friday
(called Cyber Monday) has morphed into a
sales event that lasts much longer than one
day. There are often some extraordinary items
at great prices during this period, with plenty
of time to have them shipped without using
more costly express shipping services.

HOW TO SHOP FOR
a Hat

"When a woman puts on a hat, she assumes the character that she chooses to be."
—**STEPHEN JONES**, *milliner*

✳ A hat will always make a statement or liven up a simple outfit.

✳ A neutral-colored hat is always a good idea.

✳ Tilt a hat at different angles when trying it on.

✳ Carefully check the fiber content label on a hat. This will ensure you know how to clean it and, more important, that there is not something in it that you may be allergic to.

✳ Take a cue from the shapes found in your face when trying on hats. Try a fedora worn asymmetrically for angular features, rock a slouchy beret with an oval face, or sport a cloche to complement a rounded face.

✳ Don't pass up a hat that is too large. The size can be reduced by hand-tacking the inside sweatband or by adding a bit of adhesive foam weather stripping underneath it.

✳ Unless you have access to a professional milliner's block to stretch it to your correct size, don't purchase a too-small hat.

✳ Keep in mind that hats can be embellished!

····················· ❧[282]❧ ·····················

Black Friday sales **sometimes** begin as early as two weeks prior to the day after Thanksgiving. Over 40 percent of Americans start their holiday shopping before Halloween, so it is no surprise that what was once a one-day sale has been stretched into a significantly longer sales event. It is a very smart idea to take advantage of these pre–Black Friday sales. The selection will be better and the competition tamer prior to the number-one shopping day of the year!

····················· ❧[283]❧ ·····················

If you do thorough research ahead of time and do not deviate, you will **never** emerge from a Black Friday sale with inappropriate gifts grabbed in the frenzied moment of getting a great bargain. Good investigating and restraint are the two best things to bring to this sale. Effective shopping always requires concentration, and probably a double dose of it when faced with the crowds on Black Friday. Therefore, it is of utmost importance that ↪

you check ahead and see if the retailer carries what you are looking for, and at what markdown price. Then, while in the thick of the madness, you'll stay focused only on your shopping goals and ignore anything and everything that is even slightly off plan.

·········· ❧[284]❧ ··········

Lining up outside a brick-and-mortar store at the crack of dawn or late at night will sometimes yield additional discounts. Many retailers offer Black Friday incentives to a specific number of early birds. If your research shows that a particular Black Friday sale is featuring something on your gift list at a great price, why not plan to be there at the start of the sale? It raises the chances of you getting to the item before it sells out, and it gives you access to other potentially wonderful in-person-only doorbuster deals!

················· ﹈[285]﹈ ·················

Shopping year-round for holiday gifts will
always give you an edge on finding *the* perfect
thing. It gives you access to four times the
number of choices that you have during the
official holiday selling season. Therefore, the
odds of matching each person on your list
with the absolutely perfect gift rise, as does
the chance of finding the item on sale or even
clearance.

················· ﹈[286]﹈ ·················

Never expect a bargain on jewelry close
to Christmas. Retailers are counting on the
spirit of the season inspiring you to purchase
something sparkly. Even though you will see
a tremendous amount of promotion, the
actual discounts that you find will be slight.
To get a great deal, celebrate Christmas in the
non-gift-giving months of July and August.

⁘[287]⁘

$\mathcal{N}$ever begin the holiday shopping process without first creating a master list of everyone you intend to shop for, as well as the amount you're willing to spend on them. (This can be made easier by adjusting and amending last year's gift list.) Then always plan on a 10 percent overage. Having something to reference will safeguard you from overlooking or overspending. It's okay to go over budget on a few gifts, but not without going under on some others. As for the added 10 percent, if you do not spend it on additional gifts, there will always be costs that you may not have planned for, such as shipping, gift wrapping, and so on.

·························· ❧[288]❧ ··························

$\mathcal{A}$lways keep a list of what you've previously given your friends and family. This will ensure that you are not repeating gifts or beating to death what was once a great variation on a theme. Tracking prior presents is also a great way to coordinate future gifts.

·························· ❧[289]❧ ··························

If you're at a total loss shopping for someone you buy for year-to-year, starting a collection is always a great way to keep gifts special. Good gift giving is an art, and finding the perfect thing that completely captures someone is a magnificent accomplishment. Over many years, however, it can get harder to keep it fresh and exciting. If you are at that place, it may be the time to start a collection that reflects his or her personal style. Build it around a favorite gemstone, team, or culture and you will create a wonderful framework that you (and others) can add to every year.

·········· ⊱[290]⊰ ··········

Never forget that you are shopping for someone else's taste. Stick with asking yourself if *she* will like something, not whether *you* do or not. Every person is completely unique, and what is beautiful to some is downright hideous to others. There is a very good chance that there is a person on your holiday gift list with a completely different style from yours. As *she* will be the person using or wearing the present, try to honor her personal style, and resist imprinting her with yours!

·········· ⊱[291]⊰ ··········

When shopping for a friend, always pay attention to the visual clues of his current wardrobe. It will inform you as to what colors, cut, pattern, fit, and fabric work for him, and will give you some assurance that your gift will be appropriate to his style.

········· ⚜[292]⚜ ·········

Never pay for online shipping during the holidays. There is so much competition for your business that you never have to pay for shipping during this time of the year. If a site doesn't offer free shipping, get in touch with customer service and tell the representative you will purchase on another site if the company won't waive the shipping. Nine times out of ten, the company will be happy to accommodate you.

········· ⚜[293]⚜ ·········

Holiday (or any-time) gifts can always be gift wrapped and shipped directly to the recipient, saving you the time of wrapping and shipping yourself! For a nominal fee, both online and brick-and-mortar retailers offer inexpensive gift-wrapping services. The time you would have spent doing this is often better used finishing up your holiday shopping or finding a gift for yourself.

········· ⁂[294]⁂ ·········

You can *always* maximize your holiday shopping time by having your gifts wrapped at a charity gift-wrap booth in your local mall or shopping center. Not only can you feel good about helping out a nonprofit organization, but you can repurpose the time you would have spent wrapping with second sweeps for those remaining hard-to-find presents on your list. You might even want to get in the habit of storing holiday gifts in the trunk of your car, in the advent of stumbling upon a pop-up holiday gift-wrapping service!

········· ⁂[295]⁂ ·········

If receiving a package is inconvenient, opt for the "buy online, pick up in-store" option and *always* avoid long holiday checkout lines. If you order something online and cannot receive it at your home or office, have it sent to the brand's nearby brick-and-mortar store. Not only does this option save you from waiting in a checkout line to pay for it, but it guarantees against the item being out of stock at that location.

HOW TO SHOP FOR
Your Man

"I know what I like and will often ask for a specific item as a gift, but what I really love, though, is the well-chosen surprise present that I did not know that I needed!"
—**CAMERON MATHISON**, *Special Contributor,*
Good Morning America

* Keep his taste in mind. You can elevate his style, but don't try to completely change it.

* Check his closet for sizes before you set out.

* Don't ever buy him something uncomfortable.

* Bring photos from magazines for inspiration.

* Men typically like items that will last a long time. Avoid trendy or flashy items, and think of shopping items that convey a feeling of long-lasting quality.

* Take shopping cues from a man's current closet, specifically the items that he has purchased for himself. Typically these are the styles that connect with the most authentic parts of his personality.

* Shopping an updated version of something a man already owns, rather than purchasing something in a category that he has never experienced, ensures a greater success rate. He will understand it and wear it. If he likes a classic silhouette in jeans, shop the same cut in corduroy rather than going for a carpenter or skinny style.

---

* Don't assume the waist size of a man's jeans will translate to dress slacks, as men sometimes wear their jeans lower than their waist. Approximately two additional inches should be added to ensure the proper fit of the slacks.

---

* Determine a man's shirt size with the aid of a tape measure. Measure the neck at the underside of the Adam's apple; measure the sleeve starting at the nape of the neck, extending over a bent elbow, and ending at the wrist.

---

* If you're purchasing a piece of jewelry for a man, take your inspiration from the metal portion of the wristwatch he wears most often.

---

* When shopping a belt, wallet, or any leather goods for a man, take a color cue from his hair.

---

* Women are used to wearing uncomfortable shoes that look good, but men will not wear shoes that are uncomfortable, no matter how handsome they look.

---

* Trends in menswear change much more slowly than in women's wear. Consider the idea of shopping a wardrobe of fewer, more expensive items that really capture him. They will last longer and remain in fashion for years to come.

---

* Don't take it personally if he doesn't like something you've chosen.

························ ❧[296]❧ ························

Always print and save all confirmations of your purchases. It will ensure smooth returns or exchanges, as well as help you honor your holiday shopping budget. Place all of your confirmations and receipts in an envelope and keep it in your purse. This way, should you discover that you have bought a duplicate of something that someone already has, you have the paperwork handy to return it. Also, with the confirmations and receipts all in one place, you can easily check the tally of your spending whenever you feel the need.

························ ❧[297]❧ ························

When giving a gift card, *always* make sure the card is for a place the recipient frequents. So many cards go unused; you don't want yours to be one of them.

ACKNOWLEDGMENTS

Our most sincere thanks and professional respect to these talented artisans who contributed so much to this book: editors Megan Nicolay and Justin Krasner, agents Celeste Fine and Caitlin McDonald, as well as Lucia Bernard, Liz Davis, Selina Meere, Akane Nakamura, Margaret Rogalski, Lauren Southard, Jessica Wiener, Kate Karol, and Janet Vicario.

We'd like to extend a very special thank you to the individuals who were so helpful in making magic happen: Rebecca Anhalt, Bobbi Collins-Dillin, James Conran, Ellen Flanagan, Brooke Johnson, Marika Kushel, Jennette Kruszka, Annika Lievesley, Helene LiPuma, Brian Mear, Emily Novak, Tony Pascarelli, and Rosey Vaughan.

We are proud to be a part of the fashion, media, and entertainment communities and thank specifically the members of them who have supported us during this project: Carol Burnett, Simon Collins, Patricia Field, Lauren Goldberg, Betty Halbreich, Stephen Jones, William Ivey

Long, Susan Lucci, Fern Mallis, Cameron Mathison, Ana Ortiz, Coco Rocha, Carol Sawdye, and Mara Urshel.

From David Zyla

A very special thank you to Raymond and Carole Zyla for taking me on my first shopping trip . . .

Additionally I send my gratitude to my clients, colleagues, friends, and every person I have ever dressed or shopped for!

And to Chris Poe for the encouragement, advice, and limitless support of *How to Win at Shopping*.

From Eila Mell

A huge thank you goes to Jack Cesarano and Mike Cesarano.

None of this would have been possible without my mom and shopping buddy Iris Soricelli. Not even a hurricane kept us from our expeditions! Shopping will never be the same without you and I will miss you forever.

About the Authors

Emmy Award–winning stylist and author of *The Color of Style* and *Color Your Style*, **DAVID ZYLA** has a long history in the world of shopping, starting with one of the great rites of passage: working in retail while studying in college.

He cut his teeth at Bergdorf Goodman, Barneys New York, and Tiffany & Co. (where he learned to tie that famous bow!) and went on to launch his own namesake fashion label, before costume designing for theater, film, and television, where he has collaborated with some of the most recognizable faces in contemporary culture including Hillary Clinton, Tom Hanks, Carol Burnett, Neil Patrick Harris, Susan Lucci, and Kelsey Grammer. In 2010, David received an Emmy Award for Outstanding Achievement in Costume Design.

David has been profiled in *People* and *The New Yorker,* and his work has been featured in publications including *Life & Style, USA Today, Traditional Home, Cosmopolitan, Brides, Good*

Housekeeping, *Real Simple*, the *Chicago Tribune*, and the *Los Angeles Times*. He currently serves as personal shopper, style consultant, and speaker to private clients and companies around the world, encouraging women and men alike to embrace his motto: *"Always be the best version of yourself!"*

EILA MELL is one of the book industry's go-to authors on fashion and has been tapped for her expertise on the industry by *The New York Times, Marie Claire, The Huffington Post, ELLE Canada, Zink* magazine, and many more. She has been featured on more than one hundred television and radio shows including CBS's *The Insider, Hollywood 411, The Mark and Brian Show,* and *The Morning Jolt,* and has contributed to many of the top fashion websites, including Tyra Banks's typef.com.

Eila is the New York editor of fashionWATCH Canada, as well as their on-camera correspondent. She has worked with Michael Kors, Tommy Hilfiger, Donna Karan, Naomi Campbell, Fern Mallis, Ralph Rucci, Heidi Klum, Rachel Roy, Kenneth Cole, Narciso Rodriguez, Nina Garcia, Ariel Foxman, Glenda Bailey, and André Leon Talley.